kamera
B O O K S

www.kamerabooks.com

Dan Laughey

MEDIA STUDIES

Theories and Approaches

kamera
BOOKS

First published in 2009 by Kamera Books
PO Box 394, Harpenden, Herts, AL5 1XJ
www.kamerabooks.com

A CIP catalogue record for this book is available from the British Library.

ISBN 978-1-84243-324-9

8 10 9 7

Typeset by Avocet Typeset, Chilton, Aylesbury, Bucks
Printed and bound in Great Britain by 4edge Ltd, Hockley, Essex

ACKNOWLEDGEMENTS

I would like to thank Ion Mills and Hannah Patterson for commissioning the book, and Anne Hudson for so expertly copy-editing it. This book sets out to recruit as many apprentices as possible to the wonderful world of media studies, so may I congratulate new recruits in advance – you're all hired! I would also like to acknowledge Open University Press/McGraw-Hill for permission to allow me to adapt material from *Key Themes in Media Theory* (© Dan Laughey 2007).

CONTENTS

INTRODUCTION: TAKE FIVE

One: on a warm May night back in 1984, a young boy watches live televised coverage of Liverpool Football Club's victory against Roma in the European Cup Final. He will go on to support Liverpool for the rest of his life, through good times and bad, despite the dreadful memory of watching the same final a year later, when his team loses 1-0 to Juventus and fighting fans kill one another in the bloodshed of the Heysel stadium. The shocked refrain of 'lost for words' TV presenter Jimmy Hill will tarnish forever this innocent memory.

Two: visitors are arriving for a housewarming party. The hosts – a young couple, first-time buyers – have spent years saving up to afford their first home, and several months' hard labour on fixing, drilling, plastering, sanding, decorating and all the rest. Guests arrive, wipe their feet on the HOME SWEET HOME doormat, hang up their coats in the newly painted vestibule, perch their butts on the matching pair of new leather sofas, glare at the wood-burning fireplace and drink from crystal wine glasses. Conversation begins on a tense note when someone, clearly oblivious to all the hard labour, says, 'Oh, I do like your new telly,' and is met sharply with, 'Yes, we got it interest-free – would you like it switched on?' The TV is the lifeblood of most people's living rooms, even when it's not supposed to be.

Three: the parents of a teenage boy decide to sell their business in order to fund their son's ballet tuition at the number-one ballet academy in the country. Echoes of the film *Billy Elliot* (2000), you may well hear, but what really drove this young man to ballet was the children's TV character Angelina Ballerina. While most toddler chaps mimic the kung-fu kicks of Power Rangers or play shoot-'em-up video games, this boy grew up learning ballet steps and making ballet his chosen path.

Four: amid Friday-night rush-hour in suburban Bangkok, a young man hails a taxi from the wrong side of the road. Dodging several lanes of traffic, he runs towards his target and shoots the driver point-blank in the head. He throws the dead body out of the car and drives the taxi for several miles, weaving in and out of traffic and shooting indiscriminately. Eventually he is arrested by police who seek an explanation for his actions. He tells them about his addiction to *Grand Theft Auto IV* (2008), a joyriding role-play video game, which is subsequently banned from distribution in the Kingdom of Thailand.

Four scenarios, all different, all plausible, all evidence of the media infiltrating and infecting ordinary people's lives. So what? Well, let's think of a fifth scenario.

A high-flying business executive decides she's had enough of life in the fast lane. She puts her career on hold, ditches all her belongings (notebook and BlackBerry to boot), books a one-way flight to a remote island in the South Pacific, and removes herself from any trace of her previous existence. Instead of text messaging, she blows strange wind instruments and smoke rings; instead of Facebook, she does face-paint; instead of browsing the web, she learns to dodge poisonous spiders' webs. Google is no use in the jungle – not even Google maps (you try comparing one tree with another!). Three years drift slowly by and she comes to realise her previous life was not that bad after all. She returns to the City, takes up a junior role with her former employer, and connects up again with friends and colleagues. But problems are immediately obvious: the technologies are now more advanced, new networking sites have replaced the old, everyone's mobile numbers have changed, txt speak is not the same as it used 2b, and 60,000 emails are sitting in her inbox.

Did you spot the difference? Answer: the first four scenarios are believable, the fifth is not.

The truth is that 'getting away from it all' is more and more impossible – the media, in all their technological forms, provide something akin to a global presence in twenty-first-century life. Of course, many earthly places remain untouched by satellites and cables, but then most of the earth is uninhabited. The vast majority of the populated world, however, is able to access – and to be accessed by – the same media and communications technologies. Compared to the Cold War era of radio-signal jamming (nothing like the Bob Marley variety), today promises a liberated digital-media age. It is this global state of media affairs that makes our fifth scenario an unlikely story. People can and do connect to media technologies wherever they go – and it is rare for anyone (even the reclusive backpacker type) to be far away from connections of one sort or another for any considerable period of time. Indeed, anyone who does disconnect themselves from others and the media is usually deemed to be either strange, or dead. The thirst for information and communication is very much a part of contemporary life's rich tapestry. Withdrawal symptoms are endemic.

So the media matter. Not just for politicians, not just for journalists, not just for advertisers, celebrities, PR agencies, media trainers, sportspeople, spokespeople, big businesses, banks, stock markets, religious institutions. The media matter for us all – and our pets. And that, in a nutshell, is why media studies matters too (and by the way, in case you were wondering, the boy in 'One' was me).

MEDIA STUDIES MATTERS

How many times do you hear expressions like 'don't believe what you read in the press' or 'the media is to blame' or 'journalists exaggerate things' or 'pop music is all manufactured' or 'TV makes you stupid'? As well as their negativity, what these expressions have in common is a view of the media as monolithic and 'all the same'. 'The media does this', 'the media does that' – and everyone who works in the media has the same objectives, the same politics, the same haircuts, the same cars, eating and drinking habits. We know, for sure, that 'the media' is not a singular entity – and media students are far more knowledgeable than other folk when it comes to deciphering the complexities of different media industries, practices, products and audiences. And yet the big bad media retain an oddly mystical presence. We talk about 'the media' in the same way that we talk about 'the government', 'the church', 'the crown', 'the law' and other institutions of grandeur.

It is difficult to explain why the media are 'the media' (hell, let's go a step further and write 'THE MEDIA' – with bells on). After all, the media are now more fragmented and heterogeneous than ever before. Gone are the days of just a few TV channels, radio stations, film studios, pop and rock producers, phone networks and so on. As we will see, although media ownership and control are concentrated in the hands of the few, what gets produced and consumed these days is really rather diverse. Mainstream fare like talent shows, sweet tunes, 'rom-coms' and tabloid tales will never die – but plenty of alternative and niche provision is out there too, not least thanks to new digital media technologies, industries and entrepreneurs. Moreover, new media give old fare like talent shows a fresh injection of turbo-charged hype. Add together Susan Boyle, YouTube, Simon Cowell and a multi-million-dollar media business, and what have you got? That's right...

BRITAIN'S GOT MEDIA

Take the media in Britain, for example. What some might call 'the media' actually amounts to a whole array of mediums that includes:

- Five national 'free-to-air' terrestrial TV channels.
- Dozens of digital TV channels (distributed via cable and satellite) – the British Broadcasting Corporation (BBC) alone has six digital networks in addition to BBC One and BBC Two – and over 20 million households with multichannel TV.
- Eight BBC and three commercial national radio stations.
- 40 BBC and about 200 commercial local radio stations, with total radio reach standing at 45 million.
- About 1,000 newspapers, including 12 national dailies and 14 national Sunday papers (broadsheet and tabloid formats), and hundreds of local and regional titles.
- Countless consumer magazines catering to all tastes and interests, with total sales in excess of one billion copies per year.
- Hundreds of independent TV and film production companies that receive commission for their output from content providers like the BBC and Channel 4.
- EMI (though no longer British-owned) and its assortment of music labels, as well as various 'indie' (independent) record producers.

- Advertising and public relations firms targeting all kinds of sectors, with approximately £20 billion per year spent on advertising alone.
- And, of course, the web (which is immeasurable) and over 15 million networked households, with the BBC iPlayer now the flagship convergence technology.

Trying to compile a comprehensive British list is futile (Digital Britain indeed!) – so imagine trying to chart the global media! Perhaps the most effective means of classifying the media is to divide them into types.

SEVEN TYPES OF MEDIA

1. Propaganda media: this type is controlled by certain individuals or groups, particularly governments. Chinese media are state-owned and state-controlled. All content (TV, films, newspapers, etc) is carefully pre-recorded and regulated before it reaches the public eye. Furthermore, undesirable content from external media sources is blocked or edited in order to prevent sensitive information from leaking out. Propagandists defend themselves using the principle of 'public interest' – they hold their people's best interests close at heart. Yet the major problem is not propaganda per se but its authoritarian ends. People don't like having the wool pulled over their eyes. Ask the people of Romania or the former Czechoslovakia, who helped overthrow authoritarian communist regimes in the late 1980s. Most democratic countries steer clear of propaganda media. And yet some level of state ownership and interference is commonplace in many countries, including Malaysia, Thailand, Russia and even France.

2. Public service media: this type is not state-owned or intended for propaganda purposes, though from time to time it may require government approval to continue operating. Public service media therefore enjoy quite a substantial degree of independence and freedom – much like privately owned media corporations – but they must always remain accountable to the public and its representa-

tives (i.e. politicians). This requires them to *broad*cast a range of different content aimed at serving the varied tastes and opinions of a wide cross-section of the viewing population. The best-known public service broadcaster is the BBC. Most of its funding comes from viewers' mandatory annual licence fees (the government reviews the BBC licence fee every ten years or so – and no government has yet refused to grant it, though the licence fee deal is rarely as much as the BBC requests). Commercial interests are strictly forbidden and profit-making is not the main goal (except in the case of BBC Worldwide, which does rather well at selling BBC programming to overseas providers and distributors). For the sake of comparison, public service media like the BBC occupy the middle ground between state-owned propaganda media and our next type.

3. Advertising media: also known as commercial or corporate media, this type is the most prevalent in Western countries. The American model of commercial broadcasting set the precedent in the 1920s. American advertising media were exported and replicated throughout the world. In the sense used here, advertising media mean media funded by advertising (the ads themselves are relatively inconsequential). A typical daily newspaper may cost less than one pound per copy – but its price would be far higher were it not for the more lucrative profits to be had from advertising revenue rather than actual sales alone. This is why advertising media effectively function as advertisements themselves. Newspapers are forever selling themselves to advertisers and readers alike. Commercial TV and radio are prostitutes to advertising and the buying public too – the big-spending demographic being the most sought after. Pop-music videos are essentially ads for pop stars and their records (not to mention the bumper music-video-compilation DVD). Advertising media serve the public interest by giving people what they want – or, more accurately, what the advertisers want them to want.

4. Cult media: if advertising media are driven by the 'here and now', the cult media type is a step removed from the commercial bandwagon. This is not to say that cult media are non-commercial – this would be far from the truth – but they tend to carry certain values and properties that make them stand out from the riffraff. Indeed,

they may have belonged to some other media type at a previous moment in time, but now they have acquired the status of classics or groundbreaking feats of genius. Certain films take on emblematic qualities; certain albums are universally recognised as 'greats'; certain TV dramas or sitcoms become the stuff of endless repeats. Cult media are high cultural, classical, canonical, the best of what has been said and done. They become part of the furniture associated with a national or common culture at a particular moment in history. Elvis Presley captured the American teen spirit of the 1950s, *Citizen Kane* (1941) reflected the power struggles of its day, *Monty Python's Flying Circus* (1969–74) served up absurdist comedy for fast-changing times. Cult media are also notable for their influence upon the media that follow – they become trendsetters for an emerging style, sound, genre, tradition. Few came before them, many will go after them.

5. Alternative media: unlike cult or advertising media, the alternative media type is entirely unmoved by the profit motive. Alternative media exist to champion a particular cause not given sufficient coverage across the mainstream media. Terms like 'underground', 'subcultural' and 'DIY' are synonymous with this type. In fact, alternative media share something in common with propaganda media in that they have an axe to grind, an agenda to set, a political purpose to fulfil. But the big difference in practice is that propaganda media are operated by the powerful, whereas alternative media people tend to be powerless (though in mediating their minority concerns, their intention may well be to court more power and publicity). Alternative media, by challenging consensus, effectively draw on diverse cultural and ethnic influences. White, middle-class, middle-aged people are the least likely to indulge. Alternative media serve the interests of people in poverty, people with AIDS, unemployed people, supporters of marginal political parties like the Green Party, feminists and other non-conformists. Yet some forms of alternative media are not at all welcome, no matter what you believe (e.g. child pornography sites and pseudo charities). Occasionally, alternative media with an underground following go 'overground' and hit the mainstream. Two outcomes are then possible: alternative media

producers either sell out to the 'big boys' (their alternative media become someone else's advertising media) or they desperately try to protect their property against mainstream interests. If the latter wins the day, this may well open up a 'best-of-both-worlds' path through to cult media status.

6. Social media: this type is the least overtly public (its key point of departure from the alternative type), though social media are by no means private either. Traditional forms like the telegram and telephone provided neat, two-way communication, and were not really like other types of media at all. But the internet and mobile phones have changed that. Social media today are among the most popular types. Social networking sites, message boards, blogs and other forums for user-generated content (UGC) enable ease of communication between groups of people of different backgrounds from different parts of the world. Why watch TV when you can interact with online friends and acquaintances inside your own personalised media bubble? Changes in social media in the last few years have been truly astonishing. But talk of a digital revolution in media communications may be overstating the case. Social media may allow us to connect with people on a grander and more public scale than we could possibly have imagined in the pre-internet age, but the profit-driven interests of advertising media brandish their claws in our direction all the same. Every move we make on the web is recorded for the benefit of personalised database marketing agendas. The books we buy, the food we eat, the jobs we do, the places we go, the cars we drive, the towns we live in, the videos and blogs we post, all this personal data and much, much more is at the mercy of corporate interests. The fantastic interactivity of social media offers opportunities and threats in equal measure.

7. Psychic media: clairvoyance, telepathy, spiritual mediums, fortune-telling, Ouija boards, you know the score. Yes, our final type is not the sort of thing we'd usually bracket together with the media today. But the psychic media type is the root of all fears about evil and malign media effects on human behaviour. Video games mesmerise us into irrational acts of violence; movie 'weepies' leave us helplessly in tears; travel shows carry us vicariously from

one exotic location to another; music has a strangely emotional and hypnotic effect on us. Media technologies of every kind, no matter how sophisticated they may be, cast a psychic media spell on all who come in contact with them. The very act of transmitting messages over vast distances has an oddly psychic quality. The influence of media celebrities on people's identities may also be explained in psychic terms. Celebrities provide us with simulated role models of how to be successful, how to dress, how to sing, how to act, how to spend money and so on. We project ourselves onto them, we feel compelled to aspire to their riches. Celebrities are today's divine prophets – and what they say, sing and do are today's sermons, hymns and parables. Indeed, the whole history of the media is wrapped up in psychic resonances and undertones. When technologies like cinema, radio and TV first entered people's lives, they became adorned with magical and mystical powers – and people treated as gospel everything they heard and witnessed. And psychic media are wrapped up in the whole history of media studies too.

A BRIEF HISTORY OF MEDIA STUDIES

Media studies proper began life about a century ago. The late-nineteenth and early-twentieth centuries witnessed the expansion of mass-circulation newspapers and advertising, the beginnings of popular cinema and recorded (gramophone) music, and the invention of the radio and telephone among other media developments. At about the same time, several universities based in the United States and Canada began researching the political, psychological and social consequences of these mass-produced, mass-distributed, mass-consumed media. But North American researchers used the term 'communication' rather than 'media' studies to define their subject. 'Communication' embraced both the mediated and interpersonal variety – and social scientists wanted to know whether and how the media impinged upon people's lives, communities, conversations, relationships and attitudes to the world beyond their horizons.

Mass communication research expanded rapidly between the two world wars. Before the 1940s, academic and public opinion generally agreed that the media were very powerful agents, able to influence and change people's beliefs about important matters such as politics and religion. The spectacular power of media propaganda in Nazi Germany during the 1930s seemed to prove precisely this. But, by the middle of the twentieth century, a new generation of academics began to challenge previous assumptions, instead claiming that the media were limited in their effects, and that interpersonal communication was still more significant in opinion formation. Forget the TV – teachers and parents were still the real agents of influence. More recently, a happy consensus has grown up around moderate media effects – yes, the media do make a difference, but their influence should not be overstated – and the North American communication studies tradition has experienced something of a rebirth, thanks to spiralling concerns about the effects of the internet. Like TV and radio before it, the internet has split the academy, with one side of the debate considering it a potent (and potentially manipulative) tool of social change, and the other side treating it as a harmless addition to the information and entertainment mix.

Media studies in the British and European context has experienced a very different history from its North American counterpart. Instead of communication and social science, European media studies became absorbed into the humanities – especially the study of mass culture and literature. The empirical study of the media (surveys, experiments, interviewing, etc) was largely left to those across the pond. European intellectuals, by contrast, theorised and scrutinised the media in the same way that they studied poetry, novels, the theatre, classical music and so on. The emergence of what is known as 'cultural studies' is particularly associated with a British academic tradition grounded in critical theory, with Karl Marx and Sigmund Freud as the central protagonists. Media studies and cultural studies have been largely indistinguishable since their inceptions in Britain. And for the last 50 years or so the North American communication and the European cultural studies traditions have gradually left their intellectual mark on one another.

Media studies as a subject taught in universities, schools and colleges has mushroomed in importance and popularity since the first courses appeared in the 1960s and 1970s. Despite occasional dips and troughs, the 1980s, the 1990s and the first decade of the twenty-first century brought rapid growth spurts. It is now increasingly common for people working in the media to have an academic qualification in the subject. However, a stigma still hangs over media studies (and several other academic subjects) because some commentators (including academics and teachers of other subjects) label it as a 'soft subject', a 'Mickey Mouse course', a 'doss-house degree', a 'one-way ticket to unemployment'. The latter statement is actually untrue – media studies has an excellent employability record – and the others are highly debatable, to say the least. Mathematics and the physical sciences are hard subjects, it is true, but there is no pedagogical reason why media studies is any softer than subjects similarly based in the humanities and social sciences, like literature, history and psychology, for instance.

Right now, media studies is firmly engrossed in the ever-changing landscape of social media. Indeed, internet studies is now almost a distinct subject of its own. This follows on from recent tendencies to separate media studies into television studies, radio studies, journalism studies and so on, rather than use the generic term. But media studies is still the grand total of all these newly named parts (whereas film studies, on the other hand, has always lived somewhat apart from media studies because of its different theoretical and methodological emphases). And there's still a hell of a lot of merit in studying the whole media mix – not just one medium or another – because we all ultimately operate in a mixed-up, multi-media environment. So long live *media* studies!

Rather than a name change, perhaps the most pressing issue for media studies is the promised union of media theory and media practice. The two have hardly been united up until recently. But revelations of present-day media distortion and falsehood coupled with persuasive demands for institutionalised professionalism in journalism, in addition to other aspects of media ethical practice (see Nick Davies's tour de force *Flat Earth News*, published in 2008) and timely calls to perk up the real-world applicability of academic media discourse, suggest the great divide may be closing up. All the great professionals – doctors, lawyers, teachers, engineers, accountants, architects and the like – require theory to do their jobs well. You even need theory to drive a car! And journalists should not be immune from theoretical rigour and responsibility either. Plus, uniting best theory and best practice would lay bare the reasons why media studies matters so much – theoretical, practical, policy-related, political, economic, social, cultural, geographical, psychological, legal, ethical, moral, logical, commonsensical. This media studies guide casts the widest possible net over theorists and practitioners, present and future, in the hope of catching both.

THE MEDIUM IS THE MESSAGE

'The medium is the message' is perhaps the most famous one-liner in the history of media studies. And the man who said it – Canadian philosopher Marshall McLuhan – is probably the most famous media thinker who ever lived. At the height of his fame he was appearing on chat shows, in *Playboy* magazine and in a cameo role in Woody Allen's critically acclaimed *Annie Hall* (1977). What was his claim to fame? Put simply, McLuhan was the first intellectual to take the media seriously in its capacity to shape the course of human history. McLuhan's medium theory states that any advanced modern society is shaped by the various media technologies available to it. Media have powerful effects on societies. Moreover, these effects are felt by all of us, mostly for our own good. Media become extensions of ourselves, extensions of our human senses and capabilities. The mobile phone as a technology, for example, extends our sense of hearing and ability to communicate with people beyond our immediate environment (some people are even blessed with a 'telephone voice', though few of them work in call centres). So what matters is not the content or properties of media technologies but the technologies themselves. Before we analyse what the media do and say to us, therefore, McLuhan argues that we need to know how they do it and say it.

Take the internet, for instance. It matters not whether we are updating our Facebook profiles, speaking to each other through Skype, checking our email inboxes or whatever. What matters is the medium, not the message, because, as McLuhan writes in *Understanding Media* (1964), 'the message of any medium or technology is the change of scale or pace or pattern that it introduces into human affairs'.[1] In other words, the most important message contained in any medium is how that medium impacts on our lives. The internet, by extension, is an electrical medium that provides access to trillions and trillions of pages of audio-visual material – aka the worldwide web – across vast distances. What the web contains is inconsequential to the grander scheme of things in which the internet has transformed patterns of leisure, domestic life and education, as well as trade and employment through the growth of new media and IT industries – aka 'the digital economy'.

HOT AND COLD MEDIA

According to McLuhan, the media technologies that so decisively shape our lives and extend our human faculties are served up in two forms: hot and cold. Hot media are rich in information and so require little work from our senses of sight, sound and so on. By contrast, cold media are information-poor and make our senses work harder to receive their messages. So a photograph is hotter than a cartoon; a CD is hotter than a vinyl record; high-definition television (HDTV) is hotter than standard TV. Films shown on cinema screens, on the whole, are hotter than TV shows because of the higher quality celluloid, digital and projection technologies that go into feature-film production and exhibition.

These differing temperatures in media technologies determine how we use and learn from them. Hot media are user-friendly but easily forgotten and highly disposable entertainment forms; cold media, on the other hand, foster learning because they require higher levels of sensory participation, concentration and literacy skills. McLuhan's hot-cold argument is intriguing, but if we take ease of information to be about speed as well as sensory perception, it does not always provide clear-cut examples. The internet, for instance, requires higher levels of sensory participation (including computer-literacy skills) than TV in one sense, but in another sense – speed of information – requires less participation. If I want to see the news headlines, the internet is likely to involve the least participation in terms of time because TV news headlines only appear at intervals (usually every 15 minutes on rolling news channels). So the internet is a cooler medium than TV in one sense and a hotter medium in another. In principle, though, McLuhan makes a compelling case for the fundamental importance of media 'heat' in determining how we perceive and learn about the world around us.

THE AGE OF RETRIBALISATION

'The medium is the message' is not just a statement about today's media. McLuhan suggests the media have done no less than steer the course of history and civilisation. He identifies three eras:

1. The 'Tribal' age (before 1500) relied on word-of mouth as the main medium of communication, manifested in forms of speech and song.
2. The age of 'Detribalisation' (1500–1900) witnessed the emergence and dominance of mechanical media, particularly print forms.
3. The age of 'Retribalisation' (after 1900) has been dominated by electrical media like TV and radio.

The transition from tribal to detribalised life begins with the invention of the printing press by Johannes Gutenberg in the mid-fifteenth century. Prior to the printing press, the Medieval Church in Europe controlled religious communications in the form of handwritten scripts that were slow and expensive to transcribe. In 1453, the first print version of the Bible, which later became known as the Gutenberg Bible, effectively decentralised the power of the Church. Printing and paper technologies enabled versions of the Bible to be distributed much more widely than previously. So the rise of print media brought less dependence on the tribal model of word-of-mouth communication. Now people could learn to read and write – and for the first time, the Christian doctrine was gleaned at first hand by thousands of ordinary folk. The forces of detribalisation were set in motion – print media broke tribes apart and forged more individualised, independent modes of living and learning.

But the turn of the twentieth century heralded a new era of retribalisation in tandem with the electrical age of media communications. Technologies like the telephone, TV and internet shrank the world by bringing people closer together. This is the inspiration behind another well-known phrase coined by McLuhan: 'the global village'. We no longer live in tribal villages in a literal sense, but in a metaphorical sense electrical media have expanded our horizons so that we feel near to people and places all over the world. Internet communications reflect McLuhan's ideas about retribalisation and the global village. eBay, for example, is a McLuhanesque site – The World's Online Marketplace – with its own virtual community (tribe) of buyers and sellers located in over 30 different countries. Likewise, MySpace, Flickr and Twitter resemble global villages of users congregating around shared tastes and interests. And Google Maps zoom in on street life from Amarillo to Zurich.

THE AGE OF MECHANICAL REPRODUCTION

Writing long before McLuhan, German literary critic Walter Benjamin, in his classic essay 'The Work of Art in the Age of Mechanical Reproduction' (1936), also posited the revolutionary qualities of media technologies. Benjamin saw how mechanical technologies, especially photography and film, had 'transformed the entire nature of art'. The key to this transformation was reproducibility. Mechanical reproduction of art meant that, for example, great paintings could be seen in a replica (i.e. photographic or filmic) form by millions of ordinary people – not just by a privileged class who owned or could afford to visit these works of art. But reproduction comes at a price. Reproduced art lacks the unique qualities of original art, which explains why the original carries an 'aura' – a mystical sense of authenticity that makes it extremely sought after. This sense of aura diminishes when the original is reproduced on a mass scale.

According to Benjamin, what furnishes original art with aura is its 'ritual function'. For instance, great paintings are experienced in the ritual context of art galleries; classical music is heard at concerts. By contrast, reproduced art that is distributed through, say, the medium of film is freed from customary ritual and instead serves an exhibition function, attracting the many, not the few. Beethoven's Fifth Symphony, for example, is no longer tied to the ritual of the concert hall when it can be exhibited on people's TV sets. Benjamin felt that this freeing up of high art and culture via mass-media distribution provided a positive force for democracy and progressive politics.

Bertolt Brecht, the famous German playwright and friend of Benjamin, produced and directed films for political ends. Influenced by Benjamin's ideas about the potency of reproducibility, he developed his own theories about the political purpose of art, particularly theatre and film. Armed with new technologies, Brecht wanted to change the ways in which audiences responded to plays and films. His theory of alienation demonstrated how audiences should become actively involved in what they watched; should take sides and hone opinions on controversial topics; and should not feel sympathy or empathy for characters or predicaments. Of course, Brecht had a political axe to grind – the Marxist sympathies he shared with Benjamin are plain to see in productions like *The Threepenny Opera* (1928) and *Mother Courage and Her Children* (1939) – but, through alienation, he sought to foster intellectual detachment in audiences so they could make their own, informed political judgements. The rise of the Nazi Government in Germany, however, restricted the ambitions of both Brecht and Benjamin when it came to reproducing art and ideas for progressive political ends (Brecht fled to the United States, Benjamin died while in exile).

Benjamin's views on mechanical reproduction were taken up by British art critic John Berger. In *Ways of Seeing* (1972), Berger draws analogies between today's flood of advertising images and the visual characteristics of eighteenth-century oil paintings. However, far from being a revolutionary force for good, Berger argues that ads, dressed up as photographic reproductions of great works of art, merely flatter to deceive us. While we consumers appear to be addressed with the same sincerity and respect as privileged owners of great art, we are actually being hoodwinked into buying unnecessary products for the benefit of rich businesspeople. Berger even claims that ads hide behind a facade of choice and disengage people from serious political issues. We are more concerned with choosing the right brand of perfume than the right road to a fairer, more democratic society. In short, this is the apocalypse of Benjamin's 'medium is the message' politics.

THE AGE OF SHOW BUSINESS

In *Amusing Ourselves to Death* (1985), American media theorist Neil Postman praises McLuhan's ideas but, like Berger, is far less optimistic about the human consequences of media technologies. In contrast to what Postman calls a golden 'Age of Exposition' (synonymous with McLuhan's age of detribalisation), so helpfully forged by print media, the invention of the electric telegraph in the United States by Samuel Morse in 1837 signalled a new era – what Postman calls the 'Age of Show Business'. The telegraph provided faster communication across greater distances than any medium had done before. While McLuhan suggests the electric telegraph catapulted society into a retribalised age of progressiveness, Postman argues that telegraphy eroded the literate culture nurtured by print media. Unlike the print media of books and letters, telegraphic messages tended to lack context or detail, did not answer complex questions, were often addressed to a general audience of no one in particular, and did not sufficiently afford the right to reply. In short, the telegraph bred low culture!

Along with telegraphy, Postman blames the visual media of photography and TV for encouraging unintelligent, idiosyncratic responses: 'For countless Americans, seeing, not reading, became the basis for believing.'[2] The Age of Show Business, arriving as image and sound-bite, diluted the more cultured Age of Print. Like children, Postman claims that we have learnt to enjoy visual rather than textual pleasures and now live in a 'peek-a-boo world' devoid of intellectuality. At the same time, children are growing into adults quicker than ever before. The former dominance of print media like books demanded a schooling period for children to fine-tune their intellectual development, but the Age of Show Business is accessible to child and adult alike, which explains the title of another Postman book: *The Disappearance of Childhood* (1982).

The main target of Postman's vitriol is TV. Such is its influence on contemporary life that it has created a new epistemology. Epistemology is the study of how we come to know about things that claim to be true. Postman argues that TV not only provides us with knowledge of the world, but ways of knowing this world too. TV's epistemology is defined by its overriding feature – it is for our *vision* more so than any other human sense. And audiences see sequences of random, incoherent images (e.g. commercial breaks) that serve up nothing other than infantile entertainment. Postman also fears that TV is effectively bringing about 'culture-death'. He inaugurates the United States as the world's first Technopoly; the first nation to have surrendered its whole culture and way of life to the power of media, information and communication technologies. A scary thought, indeed!

THE AGE OF PLACELESSNESS

Another media theorist influenced by McLuhan is American Joshua Meyrowitz. In *No Sense of Place* (1985), Meyrowitz argues that the media bring different social situations in different physical places into a shared domain – everyone's homes and the public eye: 'The telephone, radio and television make the boundaries of all social spaces more permeable.'[3] This is very different from the impact of print media on society. Echoing McLuhan, Meyrowitz argues that print media like books and newspapers have, historically, retained the link between people and their sense of place. Individuals who could read print media in order to gain knowledge and retrieve information, for example, were placed in more favourable positions than illiterate people. Moreover, skilled users of print media networked with their intelligent peers rather than with those unable to read or write.

With the advent of TV, telephone and radio, however, Meyrowitz claims that access to knowledge and information is shared by all, regardless of literacy skills. Electronic media effectively blur socio-economic class, age, ethnic and other differences. Take the modern-day scenario of a child watching a TV bulletin about sexually transmitted diseases. In the age of print media, that child would have had to be able to read as well as access the right books in order to learn about these 'adult' issues – information of this kind was far less easily *placed* then than now. So where print media segregated people according to education and socio-economic class, electronic media merge us all together. According to Meyrowitz, the middle-class family and the ghettoised clan inhabit the same social networks of information and knowledge, so their sense of physical separation – the fact that they live in different places – pales into insignificance compared to their sense of mediated togetherness. This is what Meyrowitz means by his concept of placelessness – people are no longer defined by physical boundaries or places (where we are) but by networks of information and knowledge (what we know), facilitated by new media technologies that have no sense of place.

In line with McLuhan's 'medium is the message' perspective, Meyrowitz shows how TV and other electronic media are harbingers of social and political change that help to banish social inequalities. Children and adults, men and women, rich and poor, leaders and followers are no longer so divided thanks to the media. Meyrowitz even claims that TV shaped the progressive politics of the first generation that grew up with it. It was this generation that came of age in France, the United States and other countries during the radical student protests of 1968. Feminist and civil-rights movements were inspired by the democratic effects of TV, too. Meyrowitz makes a compelling case for the social benefits of electronic media, though critics have been quick to point out that ongoing problems of technological and social exclusion are side-stepped in his argument.

TECHNOLOGICAL DETERMINISM

Despite its breadth of appeal, the 'medium is the message' perspective has undergone sustained criticism and McLuhan has at least as many opponents as exponents. In *Television* (1974), British cultural critic Raymond Williams takes issue with the flawed technological determinism at the heart of McLuhan's medium theory. Technological determinism assumes that technologies, once unleashed into the real word by their madcap inventors, begin to infiltrate and dictate our way of life. The most extreme versions of technological determinism are fictional ones like Mary Shelley's *Frankenstein* (1818), George Orwell's *Nineteen Eighty-Four* (1949) and Aldous Huxley's *Brave New World* (1932). Williams argues that McLuhan is guilty of a similar fixation when he pontificates about the revolutionary power of media technologies to extend our senses and change our social affairs.

Williams shows how each technology invented at any given time was always foreseen for a particular purpose before it was discovered. Moreover, the effects of each media technology were anticipated long before that technology came into use, ruling out any deterministic scenario. Rather than share McLuhan's focus on the *consequences* of technologies, Williams addresses what *causes* them. In the main, technologies of all kinds, and not just media ones, develop for commercial, political and military purposes. In the case of railways and the telegraph, both developed along the same lines in the USA and Britain for commercial reasons, to drive industrial development by enabling the efficient transportation of raw materials to factories. McLuhan also mentions the role of railways in industrialisation, but he is surely wrong to argue that these technologies created new societies 'quite independent of the freight or content of the railway medium.'[4] The railway medium, on the contrary, contained a message (i.e. coal) that fuelled the fires to create steel, textiles and other essential materials for the Industrial Revolution.

What have railways got to do with the media? Williams claims that the whole history of communications follows the same pattern in different societies: transport communications develop first, caused by economic demands, and then come media communications (for information and entertainment purposes), caused by social and cultural demands. This explains why TV was slow to develop in comparison with, say, the telephone because it did not initially demonstrate obvious economic benefits (whereas telephony was used for trade and governance from the outset). So in contrast to medium theory, technologies are shown by Williams to develop out of human needs and intentions. Technologies do not emerge from the isolation of a laboratory and then determine human needs. TV, for example, met a particular social demand for audio-visual content at a particular moment in time. Fears about the Cold War and a decline in organised leisure were just two social drivers that made conditions favourable for TV to enter everyday life in the 1950s and 1960s. But the first TV sets were not snapped up at any cost. Like any other technology, TV had to find its place in people's homes before becoming accepted as part of the furniture.

MEDIA EFFECTS

The media are often deemed to influence how people think and feel, although if you ask somebody, they are unlikely to confess to being influenced by what they watch, read or hear. In response to accusations of unhealthy effects, media providers of one sort or another claim they are merely giving people what they want, serving public interest, catering to popular taste, holding up a mirror to society and so on. But the argument that the media simply reflect what the majority of people like, detest, say and do smacks of blowing one's own trumpet. The best measure of the public mood is not to be found in newspaper columns or on TV bulletins, but in nationwide opinion polls that draw on representative samples of actual people – and even the polls get it wrong sometimes (e.g. the 1992 UK General Election).

The truth is that public opinion – feeling, taste and mood – is very hard to gauge because it is so unfathomable, often divided and always unpredictable. In fact, the problem with public opinion is that it is not always the same as people's private opinions. We can say and do what we like in public – unless, of course, we break the law – but who knows what is said and done behind closed doors? One thing is for sure – the media do their best to peep through the keyholes of those doors, but their view is permanently obscured. Sometimes media providers do catch the mood of what people really want, think and feel. A pop song hovers at the top of the charts for weeks and weeks, a film becomes a box-office hit, a social networking site attracts millions of new subscribers, a TV game show 'sensation' is sold to countries across the world. But with each media hit go countless media flops, failures, misjudgements, has-beens, never-to-bes.

Bearing in mind this competitive media marketplace, what really interests us here are the hits, because it is the stuff of popular culture that invariably becomes the focus of concern about media influences and effects. God-fearing folk may get caught up in their concerns about a particular TV show or song lyric, and neglect to acknowledge the endless 'media mediocrity' that consumers routinely turn their backs on. Worse still, public fear-mongering may unintentionally sky-rocket objects of censure up the pop charts and box-office hit lists. Popular culture is not all mediocre and bad for you, of course. Think of TV shows like *Sesame Street* (1969–) or *Strictly Come Dancing* (2004–) that have inspired many viewers to learn their ABCs and the cha-cha-cha. But bad news is good news, so say journalists, which is why the bad and the ugly are talked and written about more than the good.

It would take another book to cover all the music, films, TV shows, websites and other media that have stirred up a public storm about their potentially harmful effects. From Elvis Presley's gyrating hips (his first televised performances were shot from the waist up to avoid complaints about indecency) to the *Child's Play 3* (1991) copycat murder of a two-year-old boy; from role-play game *Doom*'s (1993) alleged influence on high-school shootings to emo music's association with teen-suicide pacts; from junk-food advertising to online paedophilia – the list of suspects is considerable. What we need to unravel are the different theories and methods used to identify and explain these largely negative media effects. A theme that runs through all effects research is the idea of mental persuasion and influence. Whereas McLuhan's medium theory tackles effects on a macro scale – technology changes history and society no less – media-effects approaches focus on the micro and individual level. So whereas McLuhan is attacked for his technological determinism, effects researchers are accused of psychological or even physiological determinism. Let's hear their defence.

THE STIMULUS-RESPONSE MODEL

In this, the earliest, and still the most commonly discussed, effects model, the media directly affect individuals without interference or obstruction. Since the media are more or less omnipresent in all of our lives, this means we are all influenced to some extent by what we view, listen to, browse, play and read. This direct-effects approach requires a stimulus and a response – an external stimulus exerts itself on an object and causes an internal response, like fire on wood or a tap on the kneecap. Human beings, like any other living organisms, must constantly evolve with and adapt to their environments. Just as the chameleon changes its colour to protect itself from predators, so we must adapt to our environments. For example, cold weather is a stimulus that requires a response (putting on a thick coat and woolly hat) otherwise we will suffer the consequences (cold viruses, hypothermia, etc). Likewise, the media throw stimuli at us too. If the weather forecast is for rain, we may respond by carrying around an umbrella. Less benignly, if we play a violent video game, we may respond by becoming more violent and aggressive in real-life situations.

The stimulus-response model, therefore, assumes that the media are very influential in shaping how we behave and act in the real world. It is also known as the 'magic-bullet', 'plug-in-drug' or 'hypodermic-syringe' theory of media effects. The media infiltrate deep into our psychological characters, contaminating our minds and making us say and do things. The media are a powerful source of persuasion, publicity and propaganda. The renowned American political analyst, Harold Lasswell, absorbed these ideas into his famous formula: 'Who, says what, to whom, in which channel, with what effect.' Like a game of Chinese Whispers, Lasswell took the view that the media communicate their ideas and values along a chain that is destined to end with some sort of effect at the other end (i.e. on the mass audience). Sometimes the effect of the media stimulus isn't the intended one, but the point is that there will always be an effect on the individual – in some cases, a decisive and divisive one.

As evidence to support his case, Lasswell argues in *Propaganda Technique in the World War* (1927) that British media propaganda during the First World War (posters and newspaper campaigns) was more effective than German propaganda at stimulating a patriotic response in the hearts and minds of the public. The British appealed to humanitarian aims, while the Germans talked more about their *Kultur* and less about the human catastrophe they were perpetrating. A decade or so later, Lasswell's worst fears were realised as Hitler's rise to supremacy demonstrated the spectacular power of effective media propaganda, including the notorious People's Radio Sets. Britain's Ministry of Information, on the other hand, was sadly ineffective in the early years of the Second World War and acquired an unfortunate nickname among civilians – the 'Ministry of Misinformation'. War propaganda has played an even more disputed role in subsequent wars, provoking huge public protests in the wake of the first TV war (Vietnam) and more recent events associated with the so-called 'War on Terror'.

War is by no means the only context in which the stimulus-response model lives on. Every new fear about, say, the unhealthy effects of computer games, pornography, online gambling and offensive song lyrics – especially on young people – owes something to stimulus-response ways of thinking. But despite its ongoing currency in (press-fuelled) public discourse, most experts agree that there are many problems with the stimulus-response model too. Perhaps most glaring is the dubious suggestion that we are all atomised individuals, helpless in the face of a malign media power. It is also assumed that everyone exposed to the media is equally infected, whereas those who avoid the media are immune to effects (as if TV viewers don't pass on ideas and influences to media-dodgers!). Stimulus-response advocates can be further criticised for adopting a simplistic, monolithic view of the media as a dangerous centre of power, rather than appreciating the complex differences between the various media industries (they don't all sing from the same hymn sheet). The idea that media industries might be listening to consumers and meeting their desires is likewise rejected too readily. Besides, human laboratory research aimed at testing out the stimulus-response model has been consistently inconclusive in its findings.

SOCIAL COGNITIVE THEORY

Also known as social learning or modelling theory, social cognitive theory treats human beings differently from other living organisms by virtue of their motivational capacity to learn from each other and from themselves. So external stimuli and internal responses are not the main determinants of human behaviour. How we interact with each other and the world around us is of most interest to social cognitive theorists. Our environment is not besieged by uncontrollable forces or stimuli from which we cannot escape and to which we must respond; instead, social cognitive theory looks out at a social world in which we all grow up to learn certain life skills from each other, such as how to read and write. This approach, therefore, discards the stimulus-response view of humans as isolated individuals. On the contrary, social cognition processes mean that most people will develop to become fully socialised and integrated beings. Parents and teachers, of course, play a big part in helping children to learn and socialise, but the media play an increasingly important part too.

The social cognitive theory of media effects considers TV and other audio-visual technologies to be key sources of observational learning, particularly for young children who learn so much about the real world via the media. The BoBo doll study carried out by American social psychologist Albert Bandura and his colleagues is a case in point. In this experiment, nursery-school children were divided into two groups: an experimental group and a control group. The experimental group were shown a film of a physically aggressive adult repeatedly hitting a punch bag, whereas the control group saw a completely different, non-violent film. After watching the films, the children were allowed to play with each other and various toys, including an inflatable BoBo doll. Bandura found that those children in the experimental group imitated the aggressive violence they had learnt from the film (they gave the BoBo doll a good kicking!), whereas the control group behaved normally and with no indication of increased aggression.

A combination of the violent film's 'modelling' effects on the experimental group and their tendency to learn from one another's reactions to the film led Bandura to reach the disturbing conclusion that violent media affect children's social learning behaviours. We may feel worried by the implications of this and other cognitive experiments that have produced similar results. The BoBo doll experiment has been rightly criticised, however, for its artificial methodology. Indeed, some experts in social research methods offer convincing evidence to show how children often treat experiments as if they were school tests. Instead of behaving naturally, they search for the 'right answers' – behaving in ways they think they ought to behave – and try to second-guess the intentions of researchers. So Bandura's children may have beaten up the BoBo doll because they thought the researchers were expecting them to! Experimental research like this, more than occasionally, frames and skews the results. Apart from Bandura's suspect methods, it should be added that children don't just learn the wrong things from the media. Cognitive research has found pro-social in addition to anti-social media effects (we'll consider media literacy matters later). As that old adage preaches, there's good aggression as well as bad!

PRIMING

Priming is an approach not unlike social cognitive theory, except it places more emphasis on the relationship between media and personal memory. Priming effects occur, say, if hearing a song on the radio conjures up mental associations with past experiences in our lives. In other words, priming occurs when exposure to the media triggers thoughts and feelings pent-up from our past. Priming effects may cause us to become sad and depressed, or may bring back happy memories and help us to feel better about ourselves. So priming is a short-term effect with long-term conse-quences. We are not always conscious of the subtle effects of priming either, given that we are prone to remembering banal moments in our lives as well as rites of passage, and mundane as well as dramatic media moments. Regardless of their subtlety, priming effects are not daily phenomena. Only occasionally do images, words and sounds resonate with the chapters of our own lives. Moreover, priming effects are mostly mild and rarely cause extreme reactions like tearfulness, anger or aggression.

Priming research has shown that certain media content has greater capacity to trigger our emotions. True-life drama, for instance, primes our memory on a more regular basis than purely fictional entertainment. We are also more susceptible to priming if we can identify with and believe in the characters or events, and can freely interpret the meanings of a film, song or TV drama in ways that fit with our life-histories. And because these cognitive associations rely on our memory recall, it is more common for media-priming effects to tap into our recent rather than our distant memories. Newly-weds or soon-to-be-weds, for instance, are more likely than others to be primed by media representations of wedding bliss: the chauffeur-driven car, the flowers, the honeymoon and so on. Those rare media encounters that prime us for memories hidden deep in our pasts, though, are the most potent and memorable. Popular networking sites like Facebook, Friends Reunited and a whole host of genealogy forums facilitate powerful priming effects by providing people with new means to go in search of old flames and long-lost classmates.

CULTIVATION THEORY

Unlike social cognitive and priming effects, the cultivation effects analysed by American communications expert George Gerbner are honed through much longer exposure to the media. Gerbner and his colleagues carried out longitudinal surveys of people's opinions on certain subjects – the key variable being how much TV they watched. Variations in opinions held by those who watched lots of TV compared with those who did not were measured to obtain the 'cultivation differential'. In most cases, the cultivation differential was significant. In practice, this means that those viewers who watch lots of TV are found to have different opinions about the world outside their front doors than those who watch less TV. So TV cultivates the opinions of people who watch several hours of it each day, every day.

Common sense, you might say! But there's more to it than just cultivation differentials. Gerbner identified a 'Mean World Syndrome' that afflicted heavy TV viewers. Put simply, the more TV you watch, the more likely you are to view the outside world as a hostile, crime-ridden, ghettoised world where danger and vice lurk in every corner. Why? Cultivation theory explains 'Mean World Syndrome' by equating its cultivation differentials with its TV-content analysis. In terms of the latter, Gerbner found that crime on TV was ten times worse than crime in the real world. He also found that TV has a 'mainstreaming effect' on people's tastes and opinions. TV has to cater for the broad tastes of mass audiences, so, instead of innovative programming able to accommodate diverse cultural and political views, TV producers tend to fall back on tried-and-tested formulae. This mainstreaming effect cultivates a narrow-minded view of the world to which TV viewers become accustomed and cannot see beyond.

So it would seem that TV addicts make a direct connection between what they see on the small screen and what they think is happening in reality. TV's cultivating power means that it guides certain individuals into ways of dealing with the world beyond the box. The process of desensitisation – becoming less shocked by what we see on TV – is a classic cultivation effect. The problem is, of course, that TV realism is far removed from actual reality. Witnessing a drive-by shooting in the flesh would probably make us physically sick and mentally scarred for life, whereas witnessing it every night on TV, we hardly bat an eyelid! More worryingly, the cultivating effects of indiscriminate TV viewing by very young children have been causally linked to attention deficit hyperactivity disorder (ADHD). But on a positive note, cultivation theory may go some way to explaining the 'release-valve model' of media effects in which an individual's negative energy (anger, frustration, jealousy, hatred) is unleashed upon, say, moving pixels in video games rather than real-life people.

AGENDA SETTING

This approach is concerned with how the media influence people's attitudes to issues of public interest. Agenda-setting theory explores newsworthiness and news values, both in terms of how they are practised by news producers and perceived by news audiences. At any given moment in time, journalists need to decide which news stories are the most important and which ones to leave out. Ideally, audiences would decide which stories to prioritise, but this is simply not possible amid a fast-moving, disorganised, unpredictable flow of breaking news items – and, anyway, journalists would argue that expertise is required in order to judge what is newsworthy and what is not.

In fact, the findings of agenda-setting research suggest journalists are good judges because news agendas nearly always give rise to public agendas over time. Of course, another argument would be that the news agenda is not merely a proxy for the emerging public agenda but a powerful effect on it too. The news headlines are an everyday conversation piece. News stories feed the chattering classes. A young girl goes missing and a few days later the whole world is looking for her, or so it seems. More precisely, agenda-setting research in the 1970s and 1980s – notably by American communication theorist Maxwell McCombs – measured a period of four months between the airing of a typical news story and it filtering into the wider public consciousness. Taking account of the fact that news in today's post-CNN media marketplace is available more readily and on a more 'rolling' format than 20 or 30 years ago, this four-month rule has almost certainly shortened.

Like cultivation theory, the agenda-setting approach seeks to understand long-term media effects on how we form opinions about each other and the world beyond our immediate locale. Other agenda-setting studies point to the 'status conferral function' of the media – how extensive media exposure improves the reputation of, say, a politician or pundit – and the capacity of the media to enforce 'social norms' like what we should wear to stay fashionable among friends. However, public agendas don't always follow media ones. For instance, too much bland political news might bring about a wider trend for political apathy. So political apathy may well be an outcome of the media agenda – newscasters typically judge political stories to be highly newsworthy – being rejected by the public agenda, which may in turn reject the agenda of public representatives (i.e. politicians). Agenda-setting theorists like McCombs have responded by arguing that news media can raise the public profile of politics and politicians with more sustained, in-depth coverage that enables audiences to learn about key issues and policies – not just image and personality.

THE INNOVATION DIFFUSION MODEL

Let's round off our discussion of media effects with an approach that tries to gauge how quickly a new technology disseminates into public life. Five adopter categories are identified by American sociologist Everett Rogers in his seminal *Diffusion of Innovations* (1962). First, 'innovators' are those individuals who are willing to try out (and even create) new technologies, many of whom meet at specialist conventions to discuss the latest products and ideas. Of course, some innovators become very wealthy as a result of laying successful claim to patent and intellectual property rights, but there are always more claimants than claims, so many would-be innovators miss out on the spoils. Second, 'early adopters' are technologically savvy people who take their lead from the innovators and become the first major social group to try out their innovation. Early adopters are vital in successful innovation diffusion. Not only are they the first to buy into new technologies (often at peak prices) but they also provide feedback to help improve their user-friendliness for later adopters.

Third and fourth come the 'early majority' and 'late majority' who make up the bulk of the population – the former group adopting the innovation slightly sooner and less hesitantly than the latter. Finally, 'laggards' are the last to adopt the innovation, remaining stubbornly sceptical until they are finally convinced by everyone else to change their ways. In general, Rogers finds that 'earlier adopters have higher socio-economic status than later adopters.' It goes without saying that not every new technology will become successfully diffused across all five adopter categories. For example, in the 1980s, Digital Audio Tapes (DATs) never sold beyond the 'early adopter' market in the face of tough competition from the far more widely adopted CD. Pagers, WAP phones, Xbox 360 consoles and the HD DVD format experienced similar diffusion problems because they failed to find a 'killer app' among the wider public, in some cases due to technical problems only innovators or early adopters could fix.

Media studies of innovation diffusion take two forms. On the one hand, it is possible to plot the diffusion of media technologies over space and time with the aid of survey and sales figures. Some innovations, like the newspaper, were adopted quite slowly and only became widely diffused over several decades. By contrast, the videocassette recorder (VCR) flew off high-street shelves and quickly became part of the furniture in people's homes. The implication of different diffusion rates is much debated. Some would argue that rapid diffusion is evidence that an innovative technology has become seamlessly absorbed into the fabric of a progressive society, whereas others (laggards no less!) may prefer to celebrate sluggish diffusion as evidence of people's resistance to rampant consumerism (theories of consumer power are discussed in more depth next).

On the other hand, the innovation diffusion model can be used to study news diffusion. Highly dramatic news events like 9/11, not surprisingly, are rapidly diffused across the world. In fact, when events of this magnitude occur, it is commonplace to hear about the news from a non-media source (e.g. a friend or family member) before receiving it first-hand through TV, radio or the internet. In comparison, more mundane news stories reporting on events in faraway places are not likely to become topics of conversation, so receiving scant diffusion beyond media sources. Moreover, news about a specific region (e.g. Alaska) or sector (e.g. the financial markets) will become widely diffused across this region or sector, though not usually elsewhere. News-diffusion studies provide important market-research data for journalists aiming to give people stories they want. The news-diffusion model can also be put into practice for the good of society. For instance, the news media may have a positive effect in helping to disseminate awareness of social problems like AIDs or teenage pregnancies. On the other hand, negative media effects would be evident if people started to adopt racist views on receiving unfavourable reports about immigration rates.

CONSUMER POWER

In stark contrast to media effects are perspectives on consumer power. Now the emphasis shifts from the media to the audience; from effects to uses; from exploited to elusive consumers; from alienated masses to resistant individuals. The media industries are ideal for testing out consumer power. What the media produce are not necessities we *need* to consume, but forms of information and entertainment we may *desire* to experience. If TV supplied us with our water, we'd have no choice but to consume it. But it doesn't, and we do have choice. Media consumers can pick and choose as they wish without needing to rely on any product or service for their continued existence. Yet the big question remains: how much choice do consumers really enjoy?

Exponents of consumer power argue that we use the media how and when we like, for as little or long as we wish. In a fiercely competitive media environment, broadcasters and other producers desperately vie for our attention. Many of us now enjoy the choice of hundreds of digital TV and radio channels, a whole host of games and music styles, countless movies and magazines, not to mention the seemingly infinite offerings of the worldwide web. In order to meet consumer demand in this ever more decentralised media economy, producers must outwit each other with bigger and better content, leaving the consumer in what is surely a win-win situation.

But if we take off our rose-tinted spectacles for a moment, it may be difficult to see consumers enjoying said privileges. Consumer power is a highly controversial concept in media studies. The media, whether driven by commercial or public-service ends, first and foremost must justify their acumen to clients and other stakeholders. And the number-one priority for most media institutions is keeping advertisers and sponsors happy. Exponents of consumer power claim that audiences pay little attention to ads and are certainly not manipulated into buying products advertised at them. But at the same time, the media are becoming more and more astute at selling our personalised consumer profiles for advertising space. Are we really in control? You decide! In the meantime, here are some approaches that place the controls firmly in consumer hands.

THE TWO-STEP FLOW MODEL

As opposed to the stimulus–response model of direct effects, the two-step flow model outlined by American sociologists Elihu Katz and Paul Lazarsfeld in *Personal Influence* (1955) shows how media influence is cushioned by the influence individuals exert on each other. So this model rejects the idea that the media simply flow like waves over consumers, drowning them in a sea of vice and violence. The two steps involved are equally influential: facts and ideas travel from the media to opinion leaders within local communities (step one), and then from opinion leaders to more passive consumers in these communities (step two). Therefore, the two-step flow model argues that interpersonal communication intervenes in the flow of media communication from source to final destination. This is sometimes called a limited-effects approach because the media are considered to be merely one among several influences on people's thoughts and feelings.

With its emphasis on free-flowing meanings and ideas, the two-step flow model espouses consumer (not media) power. The role of the opinion leader is crucial in framing the big media picture to fit local community and family life. For Katz and Lazarsfeld, the opinion leader is a key communications role, just as important in the formation of public opinion as the journalist or film director. No doubt we all know an opinion leader of one sort or another. They are the movers and shakers, the hosts of the party, the leaders of the gang, enjoying the gift of the gab. In bygone times, religious leaders filled this role, but in today's increasingly secularised communities the opinion-leader type is less predictable. Professionals like teachers and doctors are often opinion leaders, but so can be publicans and shopkeepers, bus drivers and check-out assistants, next-door neighbours, mums and dads, brothers and sisters, friends and colleagues, practically anyone. These plentiful opinion leaders, in theory at least, build buffers between media effects and unadulterated media consumption.

Another seminal study of interpersonal communication is American sociologist Joseph Klapper's *The Effects of Mass Communication* (1960). Klapper presents evidence to prove that the media only reinforce people's existing opinions and don't brainwash them with new ones. This explains why our predisposed opinions influence, say, our choice of newspaper or radio station. Conservative voters buy Conservative newspapers because the editorials accord with their politics. Likewise, the predispositions of the group to which they belong (family and friends) have a key bearing on their opinions, as do opinion leaders outside of these groups. Klapper also doubts the progressive potential of the media to alter the public mood, given that commercial press and broadcasters follow tried-and-trusted formulae, so averting the risk of alienating advertisers and audiences with more challenging, original content.

USES AND GRATIFICATIONS THEORY

The argument underpinning this approach is that audiences use the media – not vice versa. Uses and gratifications theory moves away from fears of effects to fulfilment of needs. The theory goes like this. Human beings are deemed to have various social and psychological needs. These needs generate certain expectations of the media (as well as of the food we eat, the car we drive, etc) that are then sought out and selected in order to realise those expectations, resulting in needs gratifications. An obvious analogy would be the act of eating a meal when we need to satisfy our hunger, and the subsequent gratification we experience if the meal meets our expectations. Likewise, we play video games or watch stand-up comedy on TV in order to gratify our need for excitement or laughter. The need always precedes the effect, meaning that media effects are self-regulated, wholly beneficial and tailored to our temporal moods and whims.

So uses and gratifications theory treats audiences as active and intelligent in their media choices and uses. It also reverses the assumption made by effects studies that audiences are held captive by the media. Instead, the media are like a set of tools that consumers freely utilise at any time to fix any necessity. Media technologies may even fulfil consumer needs in relatively superficial ways when, say, we turn on the radio as a soundtrack to ironing our clothes. In this case, the radio helps to reduce boredom by gratifying the need for something interesting to which we may listen. We may also use violent video games to gratify the need to release some pent-up aggression. Unbeknownst to us, video games may serve a vital release-valve function in preventing us from throwing our fists at people in our real lives. It seems the media and its consumers can do no wrong!

The optimism espoused by uses and gratifications theory is not without its critics, though. One major criticism is a lack of consensus about what the most basic human needs actually are, and whether these needs are universal or vary on an individual or cultural basis. The idea that media products are always able to satisfy consumer expectations is also questionable, and smacks of an uncritical defence of the media. Surely the media sometimes fall short of our needs and expectations when, for instance, we face a barrage of advertising in our email inbox or buy a ticket to the latest blockbuster movie and leave disappointed?

CONSUMER RESISTANCE

The resistance approach makes the case for audiences routinely opposing the wishes and intentions of media institutions. According to this approach, consumers routinely redefine the uses and meanings of media products in ways unanticipated by producers. For instance, teenagers reinvent lyrics to their favourite pop songs or besiege expensive clothing brands like Burberry by turning them into fads (often with the help of forgeries). These unpredictable resistance tactics ultimately diminish the reputations of products and brands across the wider consumer market. Media 'flops' are further evidence of consumer resistance, like the lame *Thunderbirds* (2004) and the heavy loss-making *Catwoman* (2004) – as well as most films starring Jennifer Lopez.

The resistance theories of British media scholar John Fiske (see *Understanding Popular Culture*, 1989) are especially complicit with consumer power. Fiske refers to two media economies: one financial, the other cultural. The financial economy is the domain of media producers – this is the business end of the media. Advertising is the main drive. Audiences are merely commodities and statistics used by the financial economy to attract advertising revenue. In direct combat with the financial is the cultural economy – the consumer end of things. The cultural economy is about meanings and pleasures generated by active consumers, oblivious to the profit-making intentions of the financial economy. Audiences are no longer commodities but living, breathing networks of resistant individuals. According to Fiske, it is from within this cultural economy that popular culture is made. The media can throw at consumers all manner of shows, games, celebrities, movies and so on, but only consumers can judge what becomes popular (i.e. profitable) and does not.

Fiske sees consumers and producers constantly locked in this eternal battle of wits, which explains why it is often difficult to predict the latest 'hit' or 'flop'. Market research aims to find out what people want, but consumer surveys rarely reflect what people say and do in practice. However, Fiske claims there is a common thread running through media products that consumers endorse as popular culture. All popular music, hit TV shows and so on allow consumers to play with their meanings, appropriating them for their own ends in the temporal ebbs and flows of their daily lives. In other words, popular cultural media offer a range of alternative pleasures and uses that resist the profit-driven agendas of media producers.

A good example of a popular and open-ended media product, Fiske argues, is Madonna. Madonna as 'pop star' in the cultural economy enables her fans to identify with her subversive feminist and bisexual agenda. In the financial economy, of course, Madonna is merely a vehicle for selling millions of CDs as well as DVDs, concert tickets, merchandise and so on. But to her fans in the cultural economy, Madonna is a figurehead in their struggles to erode the patriarchal structures in many societies that oppress young women, lesbian, gay and bisexual people.

Consumer resistance does seem to ring true in the case of progressive media examples like Madonna, although it is fair to say that the young Madonna was more subversive than the present-day one (despite recently putting some spice back into that feminist persona by divorcing her husband due to his 'unreasonable behaviour'). Then again, we could cite plenty of media products that achieve popularity without providing much scope for alternative meanings and pleasures. Talent shows like *The X Factor* (2004–) are proven ratings magnets that seem to spawn the same, bland pop stars year after year. Even when consumers are given the power to resist the intentions of the show's judges by voting for their favourite performer, they still feed the profits of producers in phone-call charges. In effect, a premium is placed on consumer power! Surely these talent shows work for the financial economy more so than the cultural one? Another criticism of Fiske's perspective is that consumer resistance – however powerful it may be – has virtually no say in what the media choose to produce. The cultural economy goes some way in affecting decision-making in the financial economy, but the financial economy fires the first shots.

CULTURAL CAPITAL

Capital means monetary wealth. Big businesses and institutional investors (including multinational media conglomerates) are loaded with capital. The majority of individuals, by contrast, can only access small doses of it. But the concept of capital can also apply to varying doses of knowledge and education – what French sociologist Pierre Bourdieu calls 'cultural capital'. Bourdieu uses his concept of cultural capital to shed light on consumer tastes and practices. He suggests that high levels of economic capital normally marry with high levels of cultural capital. For instance, a child born into riches will normally acquire a better education than a child from a poor family. And yet meritocratic societies like our own make it possible for individuals with low economic capital to achieve educational qualifications, and therefore high cultural capital. Teachers, for example, are intellectually clever but not necessarily blessed with wealth. By extension, it is also possible for individuals with high economic capital to demonstrate little educational ability at all, rendering them low in cultural capital. Certain semi-skilled business people may fit into this category (and I don't just mean plumbers).

Bourdieu shows how these varying flows of economic and cultural capital determine how consumers hone tastes for different products. So consumer tastes – in clothes, music, sports and so on – are not purely personal choices; they are shaped by the economic and cultural capital we are able to draw on. And cultural is just as important as economic capital in acts of consumption. Even if we are lucky enough to possess great wealth, no amount of money will provide a quick fix if we do not possess the necessary cultural capital to appreciate the opera or partake in the book club with our fellow socialites. By contrast, those of us with high cultural capital may be perfectly conversant with likeminded opera or classical music enthusiasts – so long as we can afford the ticket prices!

Consumer power, therefore, is not entirely dependent on economic capital. Assuming we have modest levels of disposable income and are well educated, we can enjoy a reasonably inexpensive array of media products and get the most out of them. However, Bourdieu makes it clear that cultural and economic capital are not mutually exclusive categories. Exceptions to the rule exist, but on the whole the rule stands firm – and the rule is that if you come from a privileged background, you are probably a more culturally competent consumer than someone who is less well off. This is an elaborate way of saying that rich people like Beethoven, poor people like pop.

MEDIA LITERACY

Bourdieu's cultural capital is exclusively 'high' cultural and based on traditional measures of educational competence (qualifications, reading ability, etc). This is because Bourdieu believes – and he is largely correct in his belief – that A-Levels, Diplomas, Degrees and other recognised educational achievements matter more to society than extra-curricular ones. Being good at mathematics matters more than winning the general-knowledge quiz or baking the best cake. Traditionally, literacy has been about the three Rs – reading, writing and arithmetic. But that good old institution, the University of Life, teaches us that literacy is not just about these three things. Literacy is about learning to say and do all kinds of things – and learning to be a good media consumer is not the least of them.

As we discussed in relation to media effects, the number-one concern is always children. Innocent young minds must be preserved, protected, purged of the filthy media violence served up daily on our screens. But media literacy perspectives are quite the opposite. The media are no longer a moral threat but an educational tool. Media technologies and media content enable the honing of critical skills and abilities. In *Children Talking Television* (1993), British media scholar David Buckingham identifies a range of media-literacy skills in children (aged 7–12) he interviewed and observed watching TV. He found that they were sceptical about the intentions of advertisers, demonstrated a sound understanding of formal programming features (such as narrative structure and character stereotypes) and could critically distance themselves from the raw sensationalism of soaps. Buckingham concludes that there is 'a distinct danger of regarding audiences, and indeed the media themselves, as homogeneous. Yet the debate is increasingly conducted in binary terms: to assert the power of audiences is explicitly to contest the power of the media.'[5] Yes, the media may be powerful, but this should not preclude the possibility of consumer power too.

The title of American popular scientist Steven Johnson's book, *Everything Bad is Good for You* (2005), hints at its championing of media consumer literacy. Johnson thinks that popular culture is now so complex and intellectually challenging that it inevitably makes us smarter. The thing is that we don't actually notice the educational benefits of popular culture and popular media because they seep into our cognitive faculties only gradually. This is what Johnson calls 'the sleeper curve'. Every now and again some terrible event occurs that persuades certain individuals to wax lyrical about the bad effects of the media, but the good effects only come in small doses – blink, and you miss them. Johnson takes American TV drama as a case in point. In years gone by, shows like *Dragnet* (1967–70) and *Starsky and Hutch* (1975–79) tended to follow a single narrative thread. Little effort was required to follow the plot. However, contemporary shows like *The Sopranos* (1999–2007) and *Lost* (2004–) demand far more cognitive work of viewers. Multi-threaded narratives weave their way through each episode of these enigmatic programmes, forcing us to fill in the details ourselves, or be damned and left to rot in the pit of incompetent consumption.

Media literacy is not just about critically viewing, reading and consuming the media either. It can also refer to competencies in creating, producing, directing, writing and editing. The skills required to design a website or shoot a film can prove very valuable indeed to the University of Life. Media literacy is as much about doing as analysing. Research has sought to test out the literacy skills of untrained individuals by equipping them with cameras, editing suites and so on – and seeing what they come up with. And findings show that even lay practitioners can be dab hands when it comes to visually dramatic media production. So it's now official – the idea that you need an Oxbridge degree to work for the BBC is bollocks. Unfortunately (returning to cultural capital), Oxbridge is the place you need to be.

THE PROSUMER

The most recent take on consumer power is 'prosumption'. The prosumer is not really a consumer at all, but rather a consumer and producer at the same time. In *Wikinomics* (2007), business consultants Don Tapscott and Anthony D Williams consider prosumption to be a vital ingredient in successful enterprise. The argument goes that companies need to make consumers feel like they are in control. Consumers must be given the opportunity to contribute to and collaborate in the creation of products and services if firms wish to grow into major businesses. The media and communications industries have been at the forefront of this so-called prosumer revolution. Internet businesses like eBay, for instance, depend on prosumer transactions – the buying and selling of goods – in order to generate profits from listing and commission fees (as well as PayPal charges). And it is this capacity to empower ordinary people by offering them forums for productive consumption via new media technologies that enables these entrepreneurial firms to expand and prosper at the expense of more traditional, hierarchical businesses.

The prosumer is very much of our times. Prosumption captures the way producers and consumers have become harder to distinguish in post-Fordist service economies. The old order of mass production has been replaced by smaller pockets of technologically driven production tailored to consumer demand. Unlike Fiske's notion of hostile consumer resistance, prosumption sees producers and consumers working towards the same goals. Producers aim to satisfy consumers, consumers aim to be satisfied by producers. Some prosumerists would even argue that the age-old divide between producers and consumers has been bridged – we're all users now!

But the more cynical among us argue that this is a contrived and idealistic outlook on contemporary economics. According to critics of prosumption, most of the work we put in as consumers is for the benefit of producers, not ourselves. As individuals, we buy and sell on eBay for productive ends, it is true, but eBay and PayPal take more than a healthy slice of our profits, while at the same time selling our personal data to affiliated companies (especially advertisers) for long-term sales rewards. Prosumption, in this sense, is merely consumption that makes us feel in control when we are actually – to all intents and purposes – the unknowing victims of increasingly sophisticated, subliminal marketing ploys...subliminal marketing ploys... subliminal marketing ploys... (do you catch my drift?).

POLITICAL ECONOMY

Diametrically opposed to consumer power is the political-economy approach to mass media industries and institutions. What we are dealing with now is not consumer but corporate power. Political economy – to echo that famous wood-dye ad on TV – does exactly what it says on the tin. This strand of media studies is about the politics of media institutions and media economics. Questions of power, wealth, ownership and control are central to political economy. Political economy is aligned to classical Marxism. Classical Marxist theory considers struggles over the ownership of raw materials and means of production as fundamental in shaping the uneven distribution of wealth in capitalist societies. Those who control the forces (labour) and relations (property and rights) of production, therefore, represent the privileged capitalist class who can wield their self-centred ideas and principles on the powerless masses (i.e. the public). Likewise, those who own the forces and relations of media production hold the keys for propagating the political and economic agendas of their time. Production inevitably determines consumption. So political economy is about media institutional structures and practices – and how these in turn affect what gets produced and consumed.

THE CULTURAL INDUSTRIES

The media – in their various guises – are located in the cultural and creative industries along with the arts, design, theatre, museums, advertising and publishing, among others. Though rarely described as industrial, the media nonetheless operate in the same capital- ist economic conditions as traditional industries like steel, petro- leum, transport and construction. It is on this basis that Marxist political economists consider capitalism to be the principal logic governing media production and consumption.

German Marxist theorist Theodor Adorno doesn't even write about cultural industries in the plural. For Adorno, 'the culture industry' is one huge factory-line of cheap media entertainment designed to distract consumers from political activism and social progressiveness. The defining feature of Adorno's culture industry is standardisation. Everything produced by the media and other components of the culture industry is standardised to target the lowest common denominator of consumer. The logic of commercial success supersedes any consideration of the artistic or intellectual quality of what gets produced. So the same formula proven to be 'popular' in the past is revived and repackaged for the next Hollywood romance, the latest chart release, tomorrow's tabloid headlines, the hottest new video game, and so on.

But why do the teeming masses of consumers keep coming back for more of this standardised crap? Because, Adorno argues (in *Dialectic of Enlightenment*, 1972), people's workaday routines sap their energy and enthusiasm so severely that if a song or film or anything else is 'to remain a pleasure, it must not demand any effort... No independent thinking must be expected from the audi- ence: the product prescribes every reaction.'[6] Put simply, unskilled industrial work leads to unskilled industrial leisure time. People's needs are therefore produced and controlled by the absolute power of capitalism, both at and outside of work. Adorno lived under the same Nazi German regime as Benjamin and Brecht, which points to links between standardisation and fascism, although Adorno's culture industry is closer to American than German techniques of mass-media production. This culture industry serves the ideological interests of economic and political powers by producing easy-listening, easy-viewing, sentimental entertainment designed to provide people with catharsis, keeping them amused, satisfied with their lot, sleepy and – after a good night's sleep – re-charged for tomorrow's chores at the office, farm or factory.

Adorno applies his theory of standardisation to the production and consumption of popular music, which he compares unfavourably to 'serious music'. Serious music (i.e. classical music) achieves excellence when its whole is greater than the sum of its parts. But in popular music the 'whole' is merely a standard song structure common to all 'well-made' hits. The individual parts (choruses and verses) of a popular song are interchangeable with the parts of other songs because each part has no bearing on the music as a whole. According to Adorno, the popular music industry conceals the standardised structure of its products by falsely proclaiming the individual creativity of 'artists' and marketing them as pop idols so as to appeal to the individuality of consumers.

This is what Adorno calls 'pseudo-individualisation' – the pretence that music is made by individual genius for individual pleasure when, in fact, it is manufactured by a handful of profit-seeking producers and packaged for mass consumption. Moreover, pop music standardises and classifies its consumers too. Adorno identifies two types: the 'emotional type' who retreats into their bedroom and sulks about their miserable life to the sounds of their favourite band; and the 'rhythmically obedient' type who dances and taps their feet, never missing a beat – but sadly missing lots of other, better, more intellectually stimulating activities.

Perhaps not surprisingly, Adorno is often criticised for his cultural pessimism. His argument even resembles the 'stimulus-response' view of malign media effects on occasions. And in recent times his idea of a singular, monolithic culture industry has been challenged by the growth of multiple, diverse, vibrant cultural industries. Indeed, the cultural industries of countries like Britain and the United States make a very significant contribution to their economies. Studies of today's cultural industries also reveal that they are not necessarily tied to capitalist processes of standardis-ation. On the contrary, lots of cutting-edge work is produced by creative entrepreneurs relatively unrestrained by profit motives or political pressures. Cultural industries are more consumer-facing than ever before too, tailoring their products to consumer demands, and showing how institutional profit-making and customer satisfaction are not irreconcilable but – quite the opposite – intertwined. Ultimately, Adorno's distinction between serious/classical and popular/commercial culture is rather elitist. The possibility that there exists a standardised type of *serious* music consumer doesn't even cross his mind. Yet regardless of these shortcomings, Adorno's notion of culture-industry standardi-sation set the tone for subsequent political-economy perspectives on the media.

THE PUBLIC SPHERE

German sociologist Jurgen Habermas's *The Structural Transformation of the Public Sphere* (1962) takes its cue from Adorno. Habermas argues that it is no longer possible for a public sphere made up of intelligent citizens to engage in critical debate about politics, economics, morality and other paramount concerns. In the coffee houses and social clubs of eighteenth-century London and Paris – to name but two centres of power and struggle – such critical debate and its political ramifications were wide-ranging. Middle-class academics, entrepreneurs, bankers, shopkeepers and businesspeople would enjoy lively dialogue with the ruling aristocrats, enabling them to influence the decisions and policies made by their leaders. Alas, such times have passed, and the critically minded public sphere has all but disappeared.

This decline in the public sphere is inversely proportionate to the rise of mass media during the nineteenth and twentieth centuries. Habermas claims that rapid media growth flooded the market, forcing out small-scale pamphlets and newsletters written by public-sphere intellectuals. Newspaper presses merged and bought out one another, combining their economic and technological prowess to reinforce and strengthen their market share. Even worse, the emergence of TV and radio separated the private from the public sphere, detrimentally affecting participation in organised social and political activities. Political debate still receives airtime across today's media but, Habermas contends, the level of debate has lost its critical edge and no longer speaks to public concerns. Thanks to the media and other capitalist institutions, the umbilical cord formerly connecting private individuals to the public sphere has been callously severed.

Habermas lays most of the blame for the decline of the public sphere at the doors of advertising and public relations. Before advertising came to dominate the media mindset, Habermas argues, media institutions were forced to engage in hard-nosed ideological debate about where the world was heading, how to solve social inequalities, the meaning of life and so on. But as soon as the advertising industry began to threaten the business of serious journalism, the media industry caved in and the profit motive replaced all other considerations. 'Hard talk' that threatened to upset advertisers was soon stamped out by the barons of the media business.

But more divisive than advertising became the practices of public relations (PR), which is essentially advertising disguised as editorial. PR editorial eroded the critical, independent editorial that played such a vital role in spreading the ideas of the bygone public sphere. Journalists became whores to commercial capitalism as they bowed to the PR machine, in much the same way that peasants once bowed to the authority of aristocrats. This is what Habermas calls the 'refeudalisation' of the public sphere – the private interests of a few wealthy individuals, companies and political groups are catered for by a phony, mass-mediated public sphere that addresses us as if we were all mindless fools, not intelligent and powerful consumers.

MEDIA IMPERIALISM

Imperialism in its pure sense is the process by which nations invade and colonise one another through political and military power. In comparison, media imperialism is the process by which nations come to dominate and control the cultural values of one another through media communications. In recent times, of course, American media imperialism has spread its wings across much of the world. The country's popular music sells almost anywhere, as do Hollywood movies and hit TV shows like *Frasier* (1993–2004) and *24* (2001–). But before the First World War, the two major imperialist powers were Britain and France. The French were the first nation to introduce cinema into the popular consciousness, while the British Broadcasting Corporation's international output (BBC World Service) helped to promote the English language as far as all four corners of the atlas.

The effects of the two world wars, however, diminished Anglo-French power and paved the way for American media supremacy. A seminal account of this epochal change is *Mass Communications and American Empire* (1969) by American sociologist Herbert Schiller. Just as the United States emerged from the Second World War as the dominant political and economic superpower, so it also emerged as the dominant media and cultural force. From this point onwards, Schiller identifies 'a staggering global invasion by American electronic communications.'[7] Hollywood had already established itself at the centre of the global film industry by the 1930s, but it was the American model of commercial broadcasting that really did impact upon other nations' media policies and practices. The public service broadcasting model adopted by Britain and other European countries was soon challenged and eventually overcome by commercial TV and radio. According to Schiller, one example of this yielding to American media commercialism was the establishment of Independent Television (ITV) in Britain in 1954. Schiller lamented such developments, arguing that countries like Britain were caving in to the full, advertising-driven force of the rampant American capitalist economy.

However, European media systems were not the worst victims of American media imperialism. Developing economies in Africa, South America and Asia required cheap programming content to fill up media air-time, and the United States obliged by feeding them with TV exports, effectively propagating the American-English language and way of life to millions of households across the globe. These exported media fitted well into the scheduling of overseas commercial operators influenced, in turn, by American broadcasting values. So Schiller shows how the TV and radio networks of many countries developed along very similar lines to those in the United States, even to the extent that American media exports promoted sales of American-made goods through advertising and product placement, opening up new markets to American-owned multinational companies.

The global power of American media imperialism is irrefutable, yet Schiller and other political economists have been criticised for accepting this imperialist predicament at face value. Audience studies of American TV serial *Dallas* (1978–1991) provide contrary evidence of cultural resistance to so-called imperialist agendas. American sociologists Tamar Liebes and Elihu Katz in *The Export of*

Meaning (1990) interviewed *Dallas* viewers of different nationalities and ethnicities, and found that many of them gave critical interpretations of how the American cultural values presented in *Dallas* served 'the hegemonic interests of the producers or of American society.'[8] Despite its popularity in many countries, *Dallas* was rejected by a large slice of the world's population, with Japanese audiences completely dismissing it as unrealistic and contrived.

In another audience study, Dutch cultural theorist Ien Ang's *Watching Dallas* (1985) considered the TV serial to be equally loved and loathed. Some viewers loathed *Dallas* because it reinforced their opinions about what was wrong with American culture – corporate capitalist greed, male chauvinism, disregard for family values, sexual promiscuity and so on. But viewers who loved *Dallas*, Ang argues, did not simply submit themselves to the indulgent appeals of Americanisation. They made a clear distinction between reality and fiction, and took pleasure in the fictional realist means by which *Dallas* offered them a temporary escape from the less dramatic features of their own lives.

So the success of American media exports overseas does not necessarily imply a capitalist invasion perpetrated on uncritical audiences. It could be argued that the diverse, 'melting-pot' population of America provides media producers with the best possible testing ground for multinational success. Another problem with the infatuation with American media imperialism is the tendency to neglect imperialist incursions elsewhere. The Sony media and electronics empire, of course, is owned by Japan, and the Japanese – for some time now – have been technological pioneers in sectors like gaming, animation and mobile phones. The other major electronics player in media technological innovation, Samsung, is based in South Korea. Further developments that question the idea of American media imperialism include the ever-burgeoning Bollywood film industry; the growth of Chinese media and film industries alongside the expansion of Mandarin as a language of huge (present and future) international importance; and the emergence of major non-Western news organisations like Qatar-based Al Jazeera.

THE PROPAGANDA MODEL

Not unlike the media-imperialism approach, Americans Edward Herman and renowned linguist Noam Chomsky (in *Manufacturing Consent*, 1988) outline a 'propaganda model' of how the media implicitly back up government policies and corporate decisions, while at the same time marginalising dissenting voices. The media are relatively free from state interference in democratic societies, it is true, but Herman and Chomsky argue that they are by no means neutral or unbiased in the way they report current affairs. The propaganda model is made up of five 'news filters':

1. The size and ownership of mass media: most media companies are fully or partly owned by major corporations that inject lots of capital into their various businesses. This means there is little scope for new, alternative media institutions to break through and challenge giant corporate networks like Time Warner and Viacom. These big media businesses depend upon governments and existing large corporations for consent to go about their business, so it is not difficult to understand why they are keen to report on political and international affairs in a way that sympathises with their government's point of view.

2. The advertising licence to do business: Herman and Chomsky suggest that commercial media institutions dependent on advertising for their revenue tend to tailor their output to an affluent audience (i.e. the ideal audience for advertisers). If media institutions set out to cater for less affluent audiences, they are discriminated against because companies will not invest in advertising space for audiences who lack spending power. So media reputation is ultimately at the mercy of advertisers rather than journalists or producers.

3. The sourcing of news media: we receive most of our news from 'official' sources such as the White House or Downing Street. These sources are given special status by media institutions because they are reliable and accessible providers of news. Herman and Chomsky show how the media, in their reluctance to pursue less familiar sources offering dissenting points of view, lean too much on official sources that churn out what is essentially propaganda.

4. Flak: this news filter comes in the form of government and corporate pressure that is exerted on media institutions deemed to be breaking codes of impartiality and objectivity. Given that the media depend on powerful commercial and political institutions for much of their revenue and content provision, they are likely to bow to pressure when allegations of 'bias' and 'malpractice' are brought to bear on them.

5. The ideology of anti-communism: Herman and Chomsky claim that, in the United States in particular, the ideology of anti-communism is a control mechanism by which governments and corporate powers justify divisive capitalist policies that widen inequalities within their own societies. As the politics of Western mass media are much in keeping with the politics of the countries in which they operate, anti-communism filters down into political news reporting without a second thought.

This propaganda model has shed new light on the political-economy tradition in media studies. But it has been criticised for its simplistic assumption that governments and large corporations share the same interests and aims when filtering their propaganda through the media. The kind of consent they try to manufacture is not necessarily uniform and universal. Powerful elites have differences of opinion (political and economic) in the same way that less powerful people beg to differ.

CONCENTRATION AND CONGLOMERATION

Powerful corporations engage in concentration and conglomeration to reinforce their economic clout. Concentration means a state of affairs where ownership becomes centralised in the hands of a few major companies in any given sector (e.g. the music industry is dominated by four 'majors' – Sony, EMI, Warner and Universal). Conglomeration is the name given to companies that operate across several sectors at the same time (e.g. media, music, publishing, retail, hospitality and so on). In their essay 'For a Political Economy of Mass Communications' (1973), British sociologists Graham Murdock and Peter Golding state that concentration and conglomeration result from three processes: integration, diversification and internationalisation.

Integration can be either horizontal or vertical. Horizontal integration occurs when a company seeks to buy out or merge with other firms doing the same business. Horizontal integration, for example, enables a cable firm to consolidate its presence in the market by investing in its competitors, so reducing costs and maximising shared resources. In recent years, British-based Virgin Media integrated horizontally – through its merger with two smaller firms, NTL and Telewest – in order to strengthen its financial presence in the fiercely competitive sector of media communications. Vertical integration, on the other hand, occurs when a company involved in one stage of the production process (e.g. studio production) extends its activities to other stages, like distribution and hardware manufacturing, again through takeovers and mergers. The major media corporations are active all the time in horizontal and vertical integration.

Diversification is synonymous with conglomeration. The Walt Disney Company, for instance, has diverse interests in film studios, TV and radio networks, internet operations, music publishing, theme parks and holiday resorts, and toys and merchandise, among other things. Like integration, diversification is associated with takeovers and mergers, although more commonly with institutional investment in major shareholdings. So diversified conglomerates may not own all the companies in which they have interests, but they will usually enjoy effective control over these companies by investing the largest stakes in their share value. Murdock and Golding also stress the importance of diversification in limiting the damage done by economic recession to any particular sector. So while many newspaper firms are unprofitable, they survive because they are owned by conglomerates – diversifying across several media and entertainment operations – that can afford to finance the costs of these loss-making enterprises.

And then there's internationalisation. Rupert Murdoch's News Corporation, for instance, owns TV networks in several different regions of the world (Fox TV in the United States, Sky in Britain, Sky Italia, Foxtel in Australia, Star TV in Asia) as well as film, newspaper and internet businesses like MySpace. Concentration and conglomeration depends on the honing of global media brands, even if they are known by different names across different countries and continents. Integration, diversification and internationalisation together provide the recipe for effective corporate synergy and giant financial returns. The problem with patterns of economic concentration and conglomeration, according to Murdock and Golding, is that power is channelled to the few rather than the many, restricting competition and limiting the range of alternative voices that can challenge the prevailing political and economic order. Some have countered, though, by arguing that there is no direct causal link between decisions made for commercial reasons and politically motivated decision-making in the phase of media production. English Premier League football coverage on Sky, say, does not explicitly toe the line of News Corporation's political and economic views.

REPRESENTATION

Representation follows political economy in being about media power – but representation is less about the power of capitalist media production and more about the power of the media to make meanings from what gets produced. So representation offers ways of studying media 'texts' (films, music, TV shows, websites, etc), whereas political economy considers texts to be determined by corporate institutional interests. In its basic sense, representation is the process of depicting real things, people, places, events and so on. Quite simply, representation re-presents reality. And it goes without saying that the media are very important suppliers of representation. Unless we are exceptionally well travelled, say, most of the world will only have meaning for us through media representation. I have never seen the real Bhutan with my own eyes, for instance, but a range of representations of Bhutan – including TV documentaries and travel books – give meaning to my own personal interpretation of Bhutan and the Bhutanese.

But representation is not as perfect as a mirror when it comes to reflecting reality. British cultural theorist Stuart Hall shows how 'real' meanings are never fixed but always contested. After all, what is the real Bhutan, or the real Australia, or the real Britain for that matter? Travel agents may promise it, but we can all see through such empty promises. We need to experience the 'real' ourselves. Therefore, if reality is always a matter of personal experience and interpretation, any clear distinction between reality and representation breaks down. But to confuse matters further, our own personal experiences and interpretations of the real world draw greatly on representations of reality supplied by the media. So representation is not something that occurs after the 'real' event, but is a part of the reality we interpret. Representation does not merely re-present reality but actually contributes to what that reality means.

While representation and reality are not mutually exclusive and do not convey fixed meanings, it is wrong to presume a state of anarchy wherein everyone is free to interpret their own representations of reality. On the contrary, most of us live and grow up in societies with shared beliefs, a shared language, shared hopes and aspirations, a shared monetary currency and so on. This shared culture, Hall suggests, guides us towards shared understandings of the meanings (real and represented) we interpret in our lives. So media representations of Bhutan, to extend the current example, have similar meanings for people of similar cultural backgrounds. It goes without saying that the Bhutanese are likely to interpret media representations of their own country in very different ways to people from other cultures, lacking 'real' knowledge of Bhutan. But Britons, on the whole, will have a shared view of what Bhutan means to them, as will Thais, Americans, Germans and other nationalities. And the media that represent such 'realities' in their different cultures will have a crucial bearing on the meanings that become entrenched within them.

SEMIOTICS

Given that we interpret meanings (real and represented) within boundaries set by our shared cultures and media, a method of discovering these meanings would seem useful. Semiotics – the study of signs – is just such a method. Semiotics assumes there is no direct relationship between the real world and the language we use to represent it. For instance, the word 'snow' is simply a unit of meaning we apply to a cold, fluffy, white substance which falls from the sky. Actual, real snow and the linguistic term 'snow' are not naturally associated with one another. This can be proven if we think about the different cultural meanings of snow. The English language only has a single word ('snow') referring to this cold, fluffy, white substance, whereas Eskimos apply thirty-two separate units of meaning to the same stuff. So snow means different things to different people, even though it may seem at first to be a matter of common sense. According to semiotics, therefore, meanings are always linguistically constructed – never naturally or universally real.

The basic formula for semiotics consists of two elements, a signifier plus a signified, together producing a sign (a single unit of meaning, such as a word or image). In order for 'snow' to have a distinct meaning in the English language, it must function as a sign that differs in meaning from all the other signs in that language system. If it fails to do this, the language system itself collapses. But thankfully the system usually works, so the signifier of snow (its phonic and lexical properties – 's-n-o-w') together with what it signifies (cold, fluffy, white substance) makes the sign 'snow' different from all other signs (units of meaning) in our language. Eskimos, on the other hand, use thirty-two distinct signs to give their own meanings to snow – or should we say 'snows'?!

Importantly, semiotics is not only able to interpret meanings on this basic level of language, this first-order of signification. In *Mythologies* (1957), French literary critic Roland Barthes puts semiotics to work on the popular culture of his native country. Barthes identifies what he calls a second-order of signification, 'myth', that reveals how the linguistic meanings of things insufficiently capture their deeper cultural and political significance. And media representations, in particular, make a key contribution to myth-making.

Barthes's best-known analysis of media myth-making is his semiotic reading of a front cover of *Paris-Match*, a French maga-zine, which depicted a black boy in military outfit looking upwards and saluting the French flag. Barthes reads this image (i.e. sign) as language and myth. On the level of language (first-order signifi-cation), the image represents a black boy giving a French salute. But far more can be read into this image on the level of myth (second-order signification). As a myth, Barthes reads the image as signifying 'that France is a great Empire, that all her sons, without any colour discrimination, faithfully serve under her flag.'[9] The image of the proud black soldier represents a myth that France is a multicultural land of equal opportunity – and conceals historical meanings of France as oppressive coloniser of foreign peoples. Clearly, the meanings signified by this image as language and myth are only made possible in how they compare with the vast range of other meanings that an image like this might depict if it was config-ured differently. If the boy in the image is white and not black, the image's meaning (i.e. what it represents) is radically changed.

So in the same 'semiotic' way that signs within language systems only make meanings by being different from all other signs, Barthes's myths only make meanings from wider cultural, political, media and other systems of representation. This is of fundamental importance because semiotics is able to account for meanings that are absent as well as present in any given repre-sentation. Just as an image of a black boy saluting the French flag has very different meanings from an image of a white boy doing the same, so unexpectedly absent meanings would also be evoked by an obese woman advertising skincare products. Media represen-tations that break the norms of received cultural wisdom reveal how all meanings are signified by what is present but also by what is absent (in this case, slim woman). Semiotics as a method, there-fore, uncovers how conventional media representations of slim, happy, beautiful (white) people close off the range of meanings available to us when we encounter them, one after another, on TV or the pages of glossy magazines. Representation is no longer just a distortion of the real world in which people of different cultures, colours, shapes and sizes live; it is now ideological.

IDEOLOGY

Any given ideology contains a common set of values, beliefs and ideas. The ideology of feminine beauty in English-speaking cultures, to extend the current example, is all about physical slenderness, youthfulness, cleanliness, tanned (but not over-tanned) skin, facial make-up, kempt hair, curvy breasts and – if necessary – cosmetic treatment or surgery. These common values, beliefs and ideas limit the range of acceptable meanings and representations that an ideology can accommodate. Diversity is a dirty word. Unacceptable meanings and representations may challenge the roots of an ideology, though usually they are simply rejected out of hand. But where ideologies amount to strict ways of life, like the ideology of Islamic fundamentalism, transgressions are very serious indeed and may cost people their lives.

The argument that the media tend to abide by and become part of the ruling ideologies of their national governments still applies to countries like China, where the media are tightly controlled by the state. This sense of 'almighty ideology' clearly has much in common with political-economy perspectives on the power of media ownership and control. In *Decoding Advertisements* (1978), British critic Judith Williamson makes another claim about how the ideology of advertising is to empower us – so long as we buy into the products being advertised! Further evidence comes from the Glasgow University Media Group's analysis of ideological bias that reveals how the news media represent certain groups (politicians, police, doctors) more positively than others (trade unionists, workers, AIDS victims). But all this evidence points to a fundamental weakness with ideology as a concept – it has to fit a rigid model in which dominant, ruling interests govern the weak and fickle masses. The same problems are often levelled at Adorno and political economists of the media. Such coercive governance is unfamiliar to many democracies today, which partly explains why ideology has been superseded in contemporary media and cultural studies of representation by another concept.

HEGEMONY

This concept is associated with Italian political theorist Antonio Gramsci who took a different view of the relationship between the ruling and the ruled. Unlike ideology, Gramsci's concept of hegemony captures the struggle between powerful and subordinate groups in society. The ruling classes tend to control everyone else, it is true, but Gramsci argues that they don't have it all their own way. Instead, hegemony assumes an uneasy working relationship between the different classes, with certain concessions and freedoms given by the rulers to the ruled. So Gramscian theorists believe that the media provide some scope for alternative views and voices. Hegemony works, however, to marginalise these alternative opinions by ultimately reinforcing the values and ideas of powerful elites.

The most influential espouser of hegemony in media studies is the aforementioned Stuart Hall. According to Hall, the media deliver hegemonic representations of reality that serve powerful interests. Hall's 'Encoding/decoding' model (in *Culture, Media, Language*, 1980) is a theoretical attempt to understand hegemonic media processes in practice. Hall draws on semiotics to examine how the media guide the ways we make sense of our world. The 'encoding' process occurs during the phase of media production, whereas 'decoding' is what audiences do during consumption.

Encoding is guided by what Hall calls a 'professional code' in which media producers follow certain procedures, like ensuring political impartiality and technical proficiency, in order to comply with regulations, uphold standards of professionalism, keep to ethical guidelines and so on. This professional code, Hall claims, serves to maintain the political and economic status quo. The media are rarely encoded with anything other than conventional representations that do little to unsettle existing power structures in societies.

However, the phase of audience decoding doesn't necessarily accept what is encoded in media representations. As such, the Encoding/decoding model reveals the hegemonic struggle over meanings engaged in by producers and consumers. Hall outlines three types of decoding:

1. The 'dominant code' accepts the encoded meanings of media representations. Consumers adopt a 'preferred reading' of media representations as intended by producers. Therefore, the ruling ideology successfully filters down into the public consciousness without challenge.

2. The 'negotiated code' accepts some aspects of encoded media representations but not others. On a general level, the encoded meanings may be endorsed by audiences; but on a more local level these meanings may be dismissed, as individuals consider themselves exceptions to the general rule.

3. The 'oppositional code' rejects the encodings of media producers. Consumers decode media representations in ways that were not intended or foreseen at the phase of production.

Although Hall fears that the dominant code prevails most of the time (i.e. media consumers endorse most of the meanings encoded to them by producers), his Encoding/decoding model is at least flexible enough to accommodate occasional moments of consumer power and subcultural resistance amid this ongoing struggle. So media encoding and decoding is a hegemonic battle over meanings, with dominant ideological representations (like a litter of spoilt kittens) holding sway but always fearing rejection.

REPRESENTATIONS OF GENDER AND SEXUALITY

This hegemonic battle over media representation is intensified by stereotyping. As far as gender stereotypes are concerned, American feminist Tania Modleski's analysis of TV soaps shows the predominance of two types of female character: the ideal woman/mother and the villainess/seductress. In *Loving with a Vengeance* (1982), Modleski suggests these opposite types are ideologically juxtaposed so that viewers favour the good mothers over the villainesses, the latter of whom are constructed by the camerawork as evil 'others'. Modleski laments this state of affairs because the villainess is usually the nearest soaps come to a feminist figurehead. To rub salt into feminist wounds, while the evil villainess is universally hated, the evil (male) villain is often constructed as a dark but alluring sex object who may be equally cursed and blessed. As the main audience for soaps is female, Modleski points to the profound consequences of such stereotypical representations on ordinary women's attitudes. The 'good housewife' stereotype does nothing but reinforce the dominant ideology of patriarchy which upholds the values of a male-dominated society, excluding women from positions of authority. Men, on the other hand, are always likeable, even when they are bad.

Gender stereotypes are commonplace in women's and men's magazines too. Body image is particularly typed – there is an almost universal preference for the skinny figure in representations of female fashion models and the stocky, muscular frame in male fashion photography. British cultural theorist Angela McRobbie (in *Feminism and Youth Culture*, 2000) has also identified an ideology of teenage femininity encoded in magazines aimed at young female readers. Codes of romance, fashion and beauty, for example, are decoded by readers in line with the dominant code that guides them towards stereotypical roles like the loyal girlfriend and the beauty queen. So young women encounter conservative feminine representations in magazines that teach them not to challenge accepted views or explore alternative lifestyles, identities or sexualities.

On a similar note, British feminist Janice Winship (see *Inside Women's Magazines*, 1987) refers to the ideology of individual success and competitiveness encoded into women's magazines. For McRobbie and Winship, 'success' in women's magazines means heterosexual relationships rather than career or educational achievements. But a different perspective is offered by Dutch cultural theorist Joke Hermes in *Reading Women's Magazines* (1995), in which she argues that women read scant meanings into stereotypical representations, and enjoy magazines precisely because they are 'easily put down' after routine daily intervals like, say, a coffee break (unlike novels or work-related documents that demand more meaningful and concentrated reading).

REPRESENTATIONS OF RACE AND ETHNICITY

Following on from his analysis of hegemonic media representation, Hall claims that ethnic minorities are continually misrepresented by racial (and racist) stereotypes. He distinguishes between overt racism and less intentional forms of inferential racism which rely on unquestioned assumptions that 'blacks' or other ethnic minorities are the 'natural' cause of tensions in race relations. Overtly racist representations are rare in Western media today, but inferentially racist ones, Hall implies, are commonplace. Racist stereotypes identified by Hall include the 'slave figure' – devoted to his white master but seen as a threat to civilised white manners and decorum – as represented in films like *Gone with the Wind* (1939). Then there is the 'native figure' who is dignified but ultimately connotes barbarism and savagery. This native figure is not unlike the black ghetto gangsters in films like *New Jack City* (1991). And there is also the 'clown or entertainer' figure who jokes about his ethnic peculiarities in such a way that (white) people laugh at him, not with him. Characters played by Will Smith and Eddie Murphy in various Hollywood films smack of the entertainer type.

Perhaps the most sustained critique of Western representations of race and ethnicity is Palestinian cultural critic Edward Said's *Orientalism* (1978). Said demonstrates how representations of non-Western cultures are mostly made and authorised by Westerners. He argues that the Orient – by which he means 'the East' and especially the Middle East – has been conceived by the West (Europe and North America) as one of its most persistent 'images of the Other'. Orientalist texts such as exotic poems about Egyptian camels or anthropological studies of Indian tribes generate a Western discourse (language/knowledge) about the Orient that is biased, condescending, misrepresentative and interpreted solely through the eyes, words and media of non-native onlookers. This discourse is by no means harmless either. Historically, Westerners have wielded the power to develop their own representations of the Orient as seen from their perspectives, which have become sources of wider knowledge. Over time, these representations of the Orient become inseparable from a more universal sense of the 'real Orient'. The 'real Orient' becomes discursively constructed as the Other according to accepted opinion in the West.

Said has since developed his theory of Orientalism in tune with contemporary issues. For instance, he argues that two current terms prevalent in Western discourse about non-Western cultures – 'terrorism' and 'fundamentalism' – emerged in the 1980s from Western systems of power, including news agencies. Moreover, global media systems like Hollywood articulate an Americanised discourse that represents non-Western cultures in often crude and misleading ways. We might consider, for example, the stereotypical depiction of a shady Arab salesman in Disney's *Aladdin* (1992) which provoked anger among Arab-Americans on its release. Even where deliberate measures are made to depict positive racial stereotypes (e.g. Jackie Chan), these carefully groomed represen-tations often draw attention to the strained endeavours media producers undertake in attempting to conceal oddity and other-ness. Copious media representations of successful, morally upright, ethnic-minority figures appear contrived in Western cultures where 'real' ethnic diversity is often limited by social inequalities.

Said's ideas are also evidenced by the rise of 'Islamophobia' following terrorist attacks on New York, Washington, London, Madrid and Mumbai, among other cities. Moral panics (to be discussed later) about young Muslim men, fuelled by the jingoistic tabloid press, only serve to widen the perceived gulf in difference between Islam and the West. Islam becomes distorted as an extremist, fundamentalist religion and at the same time is labelled as if it were a homogeneous faith, in which all Muslims share the same opinions about non-Muslims (i.e. 'us'). To recall that old Chinese proverb, Said's ideas certainly echo the interesting times we live in, but, less astutely, he underplays how Orientalism rarely goes unchallenged. Blasphemous cartoon images of the prophet Muhammad published in Danish newspapers in 2005 came up against violent resistance from Muslims, as well as people of other faiths.

POSTMODERNISM

As we now know, the difference between reality and representations of reality – though never clear-cut – is the logic underpinning media studies of representation. Postmodernism, on the other hand, rejects the idea that there is any authentic reality or way of representing it. In other words, postmodernism flies in the face of the realist assumption that there is a real world out there that can be represented by the media and other cultural forms. On the contrary, postmodern culture is marked by the loss of representative reality in a cloud of media-saturated imagery, simulation and nostalgia. There is no simple formula for defining postmodernism. It is not the modern world gone rotten – even though *Blade Runner* (1982) is cited as a postmodern film for this very reason – but it is about mysterious pasts, uncertain futures, mass consumerism, mass literacy, technological innovation, globalisation and populism, among other things. A glance towards history (not something postmodernists would encourage) may help to put postmodernism in context.

MODERNISM AND POSTMODERNISM

The best way to understand postmodernism is to understand what went before it. Modernism refers to a period of experimental art and 'high culture' from about 1890 to 1940. Modernist art and culture revolves around the notion that individual creativity is threatened by a hostile environment of oppressive politics, industrialised economics, rampant urbanisation and other social forces, including the mass media. Novelists like James Joyce and artists like Pablo Picasso are associated with modernism. The experimental use of montage in the films of Soviet film director and theorist Sergei Eisenstein – for example, *Strike* (1925) and *The Battleship Potemkin* (1925) – reflect modernist themes of oppression and disorder. Surrealist films of a later period like *Brazil* (1985) and *Blue Velvet* (1986) depict modernist traits too. The modernist movement sought to protect individuality against capitalist-inspired mass culture by anointing an elite group of artists and intellectuals who championed the very best of art and culture. British modernist critic FR Leavis used the term 'minority culture' to describe this elite group of learned and cultured luminaries, shielding society from the cheap imitations of popular culture.

In contrast, postmodernism embraces all things popular and refutes the modernist separation of high from mass culture. With its origins in the 1940s and 1950s, postmodernism emerged in tandem with media-driven consumer culture. Postmodernists take the view that modernist expectations about artistic originality and the sovereignty of the author no longer apply. Instead, postmodern culture is about the spectacle of images, style over substance, medium over matter (echoing McLuhan), anonymity over first-person narrative, disposability over longevity, present-day over past traditions. Exponents claim that postmodernism continues to define twenty-first-century Western culture, although some postmodernists argue against the usefulness of a 'metanarrative' or umbrella term in defining what gets produced and consumed in today's fragmented and unfathomable world. So postmodernism departs from the elitism, traditionalism and individual experimentalism advocated by 'high' modernism – and instead accepts that the superficial, disposable quirks of popular culture and mass media are here to stay.

THE IMAGE

Probably the single most important feature of postmodern media culture is the omnipresence of visual images. If the printed book was *the* medium of modernity for McLuhan, the image – especially the moving image – is surely *the* medium of postmodernity. As the photojournalist would say, pictures (not words) sell newspapers. But the images that flash before us in this fast-moving media age are encountered fleetingly and rarely contextualised. Images are both fundamental and disposable in our understanding of the world beyond the screen. Images excite, but do they educate? Seeing is the new believing, but are we deceived by what we see? And if images are so central to postmodernism, how much of what we routinely see is unmediated (i.e. immediate and real)?

American historian Daniel J Boorstin argues that the image, which is so easy to produce and distribute via today's multimedia channels, is the currency behind a 'Graphic Revolution' – a whole-sale change in the way we view the reality of our world. Although not a postmodern theorist per se, Boorstin's ideas have certainly influenced subsequent perspectives on postmodernism. In *The Image* (1961), Boorstin suggests that image-based news media falsely represent people, places and events. The portrayal of what Boorstin calls 'pseudo-events' is particularly rife. A pseudo-event is 'not spontaneous, but comes about because someone has planned, planted, or incited it.'[10] The press conference, for example, is a pseudo-event planned by newsworthy individuals or institutions in order to satisfy the demand for fresh 'news' from the media. It is a self-fulfilling pseudo-event that offers little genuine news value at all, and is more about style than substance.

The British Prime Minister's weekly press briefing is a pseudo-event. It is carefully timed and staged for the benefit of journalists, who in turn report on it in their news bulletins, regardless of whether or not the PM has anything *new* to say. An up-to-date image of the PM along with his latest spin-doctored message is enough to hit the headlines. Boorstin goes so far as to claim that the preponderance of pseudo-events has spawned false celebrities. Figures of great public stature are a rare breed when appearance matters more than personality. Real heroes of the past who achieved genuine greatness (e.g. Florence Nightingale or Babe Ruth) have been replaced by manufactured, image-conscious stars without talent or ability. Andy Warhol's famous statement that everyone will be 'famous for 15 minutes' strikes a chord with Boorstin's point that image-driven fame is phony and superficial. A whole host of untalented reality-TV stars springing up from shows like *Wife Swap* (2003–) and *American Idol* (2002–) enjoyed their 15 minutes of fame – never to be seen again!

INTERTEXTUALITY

According to American literary critic Fredric Jameson, postmodern media culture differs from modernism in its celebration of what he calls 'intertextuality'. By this he means that postmodern media texts typically borrow elements (ideas, scenes, characters, styles, sounds, props, production techniques, etc) from other texts. For instance, the film *Scary Movie* (2000) and its sequels make frequent references to filmic texts from the past like *Halloween* (1978) and *I Know What You Did Last Summer* (1997). The important distinction Jameson makes, however, is between parody and pastiche. Parody is not a postmodernist characteristic. After all, parodies, spoofs and send-ups of previous media texts have existed since time immemorial. What is distinctive about postmodernism is the technique of pastiche, in which intertextual references are not knowingly acknowledged or used for comic effect.

Pastiche, quite simply, denies its own intertextuality. For Jameson, pastiche is at the heart of everything produced in the age of post-modernism – which means there can be nothing new to say or play or show or do.

This is what Jameson means by the disappearance of individual style. In fact, pastiche is so typical in contemporary culture that we have entered a postmodern age which finds it increasingly difficult to trace its history and origins. Postmodern culture has lost its sense of the past because the past has become romanticised by representations of history clouded by nostalgia. As Jameson points out (in *Postmodernism or, The Cultural Logic of Late Capitalism*, 1991), 'We seem condemned to seek the historical past through our own pop images and stereotypes about the past, which itself remains forever out of reach.'[11]

Nostalgic films, music and period TV dramas, not to mention our insatiable appetite for documentaries about the past, all contribute to popular, rose-tinted histories of how we used to live. The real, authentic past has therefore become lost in a sea of phony media versions of history. As a result of this uncertain past, films about the present day are incapable of creating original representations of contemporary life because no tangible precedents exist upon which to measure originality. So films like *The Bourne Ultimatum* (2007) and *The Day After Tomorrow* (2004) inevitably pastiche styles of a previous age – the James Bond-like espionage thriller and the 'disaster' movie respectively – because they can't help but draw attention to their intertextuality (even when they try not to).

Jameson's theory of intertextuality certainly seems to apply to a shocking number of media and film examples in recent memory when you think about it. But is originality really dead? Are not live, 'real-time' media texts, by definition, original? Jameson may counter that, while the content of live media is original, the ways in which the media represent live action always draw on intertextual production techniques. Like Adorno, Jameson suggests that the reason for this loss of originality in postmodern times is down to consumer capitalism limiting the range of artistic and cultural expressions by manufacturing tried-and-tested, user-friendly media texts driven by the all-important profit motive. But it could be argued from a consumer-power perspective that today's media and popular culture do create the conditions for originality precisely because audiences demand it. The music charts, for instance, list more than just manufactured pop. Hip hop, rock, electronic dance and even occasional offerings from classical musicians add to the creative mix of contemporary popular music. This is surely a healthier state of affairs than the modernist run on traditional forms of high culture like theatre and opera, catering exclusively for the privileged and cultured few.

HYPERREALITY

Another take on postmodernism comes from French media theorist Jean Baudrillard. Central to Baudrillard's notion of 'hyperreality' is the idea that today's media-saturated culture has generated simulations of the real world that replace authentic representations of reality. For instance, I have never lived in or even visited New York, but I have a vividly hyperreal sense of the 'Big Apple' thanks to Frank Sinatra, Woody Allen films, *Sex and the City* (1998–2004), news coverage of the Twin Towers, and countless other media simulations of the place. Baudrillard claims that this hyperreal New York has now become more *real* for us than the actual streets, shops, office blocks and other features of the real New York City. Hyperreality is the new reality. We can no longer represent or reproduce the real through maps or photography or any other technology, because we are saturated with so many media representations that they take on a life of their own in our perceptions of the real world, breaking free from any connection they may have had with genuine reality once upon a time. Indeed, the whole principle of representation, like Ol' Blue Eyes himself, is dead and buried!

Disneyland is a case in point. Disneyland is pure fantasy, of course, but for Baudrillard (see *Simulations*, 1983) it simultaneously functions 'to make us believe that the rest is real, when in fact all of Los Angeles and the America surrounding it are no longer real, but of the order of the hyperreal and of simulation'.[12] Disneyland masks the absence of a genuinely real America. The *real* America is now a hyperreal flood of media imagery disconnected from the authentically real – but now unattainable – United States of America. Baudrillard's influential book about hyperreality (see *Simulacra and Simulation*, 1994) even makes a guest appearance in *The Matrix* (1999) – simulation par excellence, you may well think, though Baudrillard (not unsurprisingly) criticised the film for misinterpreting his ideas.

Baudrillard applies his theory of hyperreality to the Gulf War (1990–91) as well as the 9/11 atrocities of 2001. The Gulf War did not take place, Baudrillard believes, because it was won by the mighty American military (especially the US air force) before it had begun. The lasting memory of this war for most people were screened images – transmitted via military operations to CNN and other Western media – showing US pilots pinpointing and then blowing up Iraqi targets (bridges, hospitals, military camps) from miles above land. This is not a war in the sense of prolonged combat and conflict (the first two world wars, by contrast, *really* did take place); it is merely a virtual war, like a video-game simulation, and therefore this real-time, media-saturated spectacle is nothing other than what Baudrillard calls a 'non-event'.

9/11, on the other hand, really did take place. Nonetheless, Baudrillard, in *The Spirit of Terrorism* (2002), argues that, even though the Twin Towers did collapse and thousands of people died, this Manhattan disaster movie was not a real event for those who witnessed it on TV because 'the fascination of the attack is primarily a fascination with the image... The image consumes the event, in the sense that it absorbs it and offers it for consumption'.[13] For Baudrillard, the real events of 9/11 and the hyperreal images associated with them offer entirely different experiences. Baudrillard has a point here, though perhaps he still understates the historical reality of 9/11 for events that followed (i.e. the wars in Iraq and Afghanistan).

DECLINE OF THE METANARRATIVES

Baudrillard's theory of hyperreality – like any other theory – is a grand, overarching attempt to know and understand the contemporary world. But according to French literary theorist Jean-Francois Lyotard, postmodern media culture has led to the loss of credibility of grand theories and ideas – or what he calls 'metanarratives'. Christianity, Newtonian physics, Einstein's theory of relativity, Marxism, Darwinism, Freudian psychology – you name it, all these and other metanarratives are unable to make complete sense of our lives in postmodern times. Like Jameson, Lyotard in *The Postmodern Condition* (1984) suggests that consumerism – the individual desire for products and services – is indicative of postmodernism in its rejection of the 'communist alternative' or any other grand theory about society. Why have metanarratives declined so much? At least partly to blame, Lyotard claims, are global communications technologies including transportation, media and information systems that have led to the commodity production of knowledge. Knowledge is now bought and sold within and between nation states; it is no longer about the purist, modernist pursuit of great art, literature and scientific discovery.

As well as the postmodern decline of religious metanarratives like Anglicanism, political ones like communism and economic ones like Keynesian economics, media metanarratives have suffered too. For example, competition from commercial media systems founded on consumer capitalist values have forced the metanarrative of public service broadcasting to pander to popular tastes. A case in point is the BBC, which in recent years has jumped on the 'reality-TV' bandwagon in its attempt to win the ratings war against commercial broadcasters like ITV and Sky. Similarly, the 'freedom-of-the-press' metanarrative loses its credibility when access to news (i.e. knowledge) production is concentrated in the hands of a few multinational conglomerates. A counterargument, however, is that public-service broadcasters and the free press are still alive and kicking, even if their metanarratives are not quite so convincing anymore. Another criticism we might level at Lyotard is that he actually puts forward a *new* metanarrative – the theory that all metanarratives are in demise – despite arguing that metanarratives are no longer credible in the age of postmodernism.

INFORMATION AND SURVEILLANCE SOCIETY

A significant media-studies corollary to postmodernism is known as the information society thesis, which in recent times has mutated into a rather more frightening theory of surveillance society. Information can be put to good and bad use. Information can educate, liberate and bring economic prosperity – but it can also be used in sinister ways for political, commercial and military ends. Theories of information society engage in debate somewhere between these polar views of enlightenment and manipulation; expansion and inertia; technological sophistication and overload. In comparison, theories of surveillance society lean towards pessimistic ideas about authoritarianism, oppression and social control. But let's begin by looking on the bright side!

THE THIRD WAVE

According to American futurist Alvin Toffler in *The Third Wave* (1980), most Western countries have passed through a first wave (agricultural) and a second wave (industrial) of socioeconomic development, and since the 1950s have entered a third wave of information society. For Toffler, the third wave 'info-sphere' wrought by technological change is resulting in de-massified media. Instead of the mass-media production that prevailed in the second wave, the third wave is all about small-batch, localised production tailored to consumer trends. In turn, this has led to an expansion of choice and competition within media sectors. For example, mass-circulation newspapers that flourished in the second wave have declined as a result of third-wave news and magazine titles 'that serve not the metropolitan mass market but specific neighbourhoods and communities within it'.[14] TV and radio output geared towards particular regions or niche interests likewise mark this shift to de-massified media in the third wave.

This de-massification of media and information systems, Toffler claims, has a major social impact on our daily lives. Instead of Adorno's perspective on the standardisation of mass-media and cultural production, Toffler suggests that the refined narrowcast model of third-wave society 'explains why opinions of everything from pop music to politics are becoming less uniform. Consensus shatters'.[15] So the third wave is effectively making us all more individualised and less uniform in our outlooks. Moreover, our thirst for information grows because we need more of it to forecast how others will behave – and respond to our behaviour. Perhaps this outcome of third-wave information mania is indicative of marketing endeavours to predict consumer behaviour.

Toffler's argument is convincing to some degree, but his sweeping optimism and technological determinism leave much to be desired. Particularly dubious is Toffler's assumption that information society marks a 'natural' revolution following on from agricultural and industrial revolutions. This means his third-wave perspective refuses to allow for broader views about contemporary societies, including the alternative Luddite view that media and information technologies restrict choice, and should be (indeed, often are) resisted by individuals. Political economists would also question Toffler's account of media de-massification. It may be true that media products catering for the mass market are relics of the past in our multichannel, multimedia age, but actual media production – if anything – is more centralised and less localised than ever before as an outcome of increasing economic concentration and conglomeration.

POST-INDUSTRIAL SOCIETY

In another optimistic account of the information society, *The Coming of Post-industrial Society* (1973), American sociologist Daniel Bell argues that 'technology has transformed social relationships and our ways of looking at the world'[16], increasing human control over nature and transforming economic productivity. This may sound like the kind of technological determinism indulged in by Toffler and McLuhan among others, but Bell's post-industrial optimism is grounded in political thought too. Five positive outcomes of post-industrial society are that:

1. Living standards have been raised throughout the world and social inequalities in Western societies have been reduced.
2. A 'new class' of skilled engineers and technicians has been created.
3. A new definition of rationality in the sense of efficiency and optimisation – using resources with the least cost and effort – has introduced quantitative techniques into engineering and economics that enable more accurate forecasting of social and economic trends.
4. New social networks have been formed which mark a shift from kinship to occupational ties and dissolve national boundaries.
5. Perceptions of time and space have been altered as information becomes fast-moving and highly compressed.

Bell's post-industrial society is also one in which knowledge production (intellectual property) replaces material production (property in a traditional sense). No longer is there a division between those who own the means of production and the masses – the orthodox political economy view – but instead there is a bureaucratic division between 'those who have powers of decision and those who have not, in all kinds of organisations, political, economic and social'.[17] Although post-industrial society is seen by Bell as expanding scientific and technical knowledge to all levels of society, the central problem remains how to adapt public policies to these scientific and technological advances so as to realise the full potential of free-market, post-industrial economics. More recently, Bell has discussed the internet as an example of technological empowerment in the way it has transformed social networks, professional and occupational practices, economic productivity (i.e. e-commerce) and the forecasting of consumer trends. The internet is 'all good' according to Bell, although it is only really good if it is used effectively to bring people of common affinities together. On this latter point, Bell clearly distances himself from determinist views by arguing that social change is needed before technologies can change society.

NETWORK SOCIETY

In *The Rise of the Network Society* (1996), Spanish sociologist Manuel Castells takes issue with optimistic outlooks on the information society. Unlike Toffler, Castells considers the informational economy of the network society overlapping with and penetrating agricultural and industrial economies (informational agriculture, informational manufacturing) rather than replacing them. Castells also differs from Bell in arguing that whilst information flows within a global economy, these flows are uneven and don't touch all parts of the world. So while the global economy reaches out to the whole world, it only works for the wealthier nations who benefit one another through their technological systems of interconnected global financial markets. The network society is also characterised by a transformation in employment that amounts to the individualisation of work. In contrast to traditional full-time, salaried work closely tied to trade unions, more contemporary developments point to an increase in self-employment, temporary or casual work, and the practice of 'subcontracting' labour to specialist consultancies. Rather than create a new class of worker, information-led network societies create new types of employment that are less secure and more fragmented.

Castells also identifies what he calls 'the culture of real virtuality' in the network society. As opposed to virtual reality, in real virtuality the media are not substitutes for real experiences but *are* the real experiences. Unlike McLuhan's 'global village' view of mass media where 'the medium is the message', Castells argues that multimedia systems and their power to target diverse audiences mean that 'the message is the medium'. For example, multinational corporations take certain messages (content), such as teenage music, and shape them into a niche medium (format), such as MTV. So MTV becomes the real musical experience of contemporary youth. Castells believes that the mass-media age is obsolete due to the rise of computer-mediated communications – not least the internet – that foster interactions between individuals and disintegrate the uniformity of a mass audience. Indeed, new media technologies enable the inclusion of different cultural expressions that, in turn, weaken mass-media organisations sympathetic to the traditional culture. Evidence like this suggests there is room for optimism in the network society too.

However, this culture of real virtuality still favours developed over developing information societies in the way it radically transforms time and space. Castells calls this process 'timeless time' – new media technologies annihilate time by compressing years into seconds and breaking 'natural' sequences (i.e. past, present and future). The problem is that timeless time is only available to powerful groups that can, for example, fight and win 'instant wars' with enemies. Elsewhere, societies without new technologies rely on biological or clock time, and the wars they fight linger for years. As well as timeless time, what Castells calls 'the space of flows' enables powerful groups (e.g. major financial markets, global media institutions) to engage in distant interactions involving the movement of people, ideas and goods. The 'global city', like New York or London, arises from this space of flows that link up production, management and information. By contrast, the spaces of un-networked societies are 'place-based' and fixed in a particular locale, so they go unrewarded by the global space of flows in the network society.

GLOBALISATION

Although Castells discusses the global economy, true globalisation of information through media and communications technologies is still a distant ideal for his network society. But even if a global information society could be achieved, it would no doubt be less desirable in practice than in theory. Recent anti-globalisation protests aimed at curtailing the global spread of Western corporate networks indicate some of these practical problems. Globalisation is actually a classical socialist objective – but not the uneven kind associated with media imperialism and cultural domination.

According to American sociologist George Ritzer, globalisation means 'McDonaldisation'. In *The McDonaldisation of Society* (1993), Ritzer contends that global media and information industries share the same structures and practices of production as the fast-food chain McDonald's. Four characteristics of McDonald's – efficiency, calculability, predictability and control – are rife across all forms of globalised enterprise. Efficiency is summed up by the Egg McMuffin – compact and easy to digest. Likewise, efficient journalism is evident in very short (less than 50 words) tabloid news stories, or 'News McNuggets' as Ritzer calls them. Calculability is about uniformity of size, time and space. Every McDonald's burger looks and weighs the same – just as every tele-vised basketball or football game airs for (roughly) the same time schedule. Predictability of taste and packaging is to be found in every Happy Meal – as well as every packaged Hollywood thriller or romantic comedy. And control of production by way of hierarchical management and regulation structures is as true of media and public relations firms as it is of McDonald's restaurants throughout the world. For Ritzer, globalisation amounts to homogeneous production, tasteless consumption and an empty stomach.

Other concepts that paint a rather gloomy picture of globalisation include Coca-Colonisation (akin to American cultural imperialism), the New World Order (in which the United States do the ordering), transnationalism and global synergy (both of which refer to Western corporate domination). On the other hand, the concept of 'glocalisation' proposes a healthier state of affairs in which all global products are forced to adapt to local cultures and tastes. James Bond films may be predictable global hits, but the Chinese, for instance, insist on calling him 'Ling ling qi' – Mandarin for 007. So Bond must be 'Mandarinised' if he is to please Chinese tastes! Western media only serve global audiences, therefore, if they are flexible enough to meet the expectations and demands of diverse cultures. 'Global information' and 'global entertainment' become contradictions in terms when we consider the obstacles of language and culture. So glocalisation would seem a more democratic and desirable goal than globalisation – and it surely offers a nicer view of the world than what comes next...

SURVEILLANCE SOCIETY

The work of French philosopher Michel Foucault has made a significant contribution to the concept of 'surveillance society'. Unlike most versions of information society, the surveillance-society approach treats information and knowledge as root causes of social control and inequalities. Foucault's ideas about surveillance relate to his broader theory of discourse and power. Influenced by semiotics, Foucault nonetheless goes beyond that approach by arguing that language is used in divisive ways by powerful groups so that their preferred representations of the world are internalised by the rest of society, who in turn accept their governance. In order to achieve this, though, Foucault claims that the interests of the powerful need to be dispersed through language in the shape of various 'discourses'. Discursive power is more subtle than either the ideological or hegemonic kind. For Foucault, discourse disperses power and knowledge to the masses by dividing language into what he calls 'discursive formations' (e.g. good/evil, normal/abnormal, lawful/criminal). The power to decide, say, what is criminal or lawful is exercised by those authorities who speak the discourse of law and construct discursive formations out of it. Like discourse and its discursive formations, surveillance controls society by dividing and internalising its power.

The pre-eminent model of surveillance society for Foucault was eighteenth-century British social reformer Jeremy Bentham's design for 'the panopticon'. Designed to be the ultimate prison, the panopticon consisted of a central watchtower from which prison officers could constantly observe the inmates in their cells situated along several 'corridor-like' wings extended out from the watchtower. Moreover, the panopticon's all-seeing power extended to situations in which the watchtower was unmanned. Inmates acted and behaved in a disciplined manner, as if they were being observed all the time, given their uncertainty as to whether or not they were, because they were unable to see into the watchtower. So panopticism is both an externalised and an internalised power mechanism; it becomes instilled into individuals' consciousness until they routinely accept the discursive formations exercised upon them (good versus evil, lawful versus criminal and so on).

What has all this to do with the media? Perhaps most importantly, Foucault argues that the panoptic mechanism of surveillance extends beyond prison walls to what he calls 'disciplinary society'. By implication, panopticism can become embedded in the media as well as prisons and other powerful social institutions. TV, in particular, has the power to exercise discipline and surveillance by articulating discursive formations. The powerful discourse of TV – like the discourse of crime and punishment – classifies certain forms of knowledge as 'true' and others as 'false'. For example, health advice from so-called TV experts is classified as the truth in interplay with other sources of information that are rendered false – such as practitioners of alternative medicines.

Big Brother (2000–) and the reality-TV genre could also be said to articulate a panoptic media discourse which includes and excludes certain types of participants. However, an Orwellian 'Big Brother' watching over us – the BBC is nicknamed 'Big Brother' by those who see its public-service values as excessively paternal – is not the same as Foucault's idea of discourse being willingly internalised by us. Rather, we are all 'little brothers' (or 'little sisters', for that matter), partaking in surveillance of ourselves and each other, regardless of what Big Brother might be doing. So Foucault's surveillance society is rife with deception and division and, instead of information, all we get is a discourse of information that 'informs' the interests of the mighty over the meek. The media – like prisons, hospitals, schools and other powerful institutions – distribute information and knowledge through discourses that we can't help but accept as 'the truth'.

But not all perspectives on surveillance society are critical and cynical. Advocates of the idea point to statistical evidence which shows how surveillance technologies like CCTV, electronic tagging and DNA databases reduce crime and the fear of crime. Government organisations use surveillance techniques to identify benefit fraud and tax evasion too, which may not please everyone but should reassure law-abiding taxpayers that their money is not being handed out to those who don't deserve it. Exponents of surveillance society, therefore, argue that 'good people' with nothing to hide have nothing to complain about – only the criminals and good-for-nothings dislike the idea. This is all well and good, but we must be cautious of our surveillance society too, for there is a fine line between protection and authoritarian rule. Anyway, all this talk of surveillance and crime leads us nicely into our next media studies topic.

MORAL PANICS

Moral panics are closely tied to the problems of surveillance society. Critics of surveillance technologies, for example, complain that they lead to unnecessary criminalisation of previously lawful behaviour like smoking in public places. The parameters of criminal enforcement are widened when opportunities open up for evidence to be recorded and used in a court of law. Likewise, media studies of moral panics emphasise the social and legal consequences of widespread public exposure (via the media) to crime, violence and other societal, ethical or medical ills. Major moral panics in recent times have centred on fears about paedophilia, AIDS, drugs, knife and gun crime, Satanism, the MMR (measles, mumps and rubella) vaccine and the effects of video games. But moral panics are not present-day phenomena – they are embedded in the history of humankind itself. For instance, garrotting (a nineteenth-century English term for strangling and then mugging one's victim) caused a huge moral panic among the people and press of Victorian London. More often than not concerned with young people's well-being, moral panics give some indication of the social attitudes of their time – albeit with the critical qualification (as we shall see) that panics are not always genuinely widespread or accurately reported by the media.

LABELLING THEORY

The concept of moral panics originates from what is known as 'labelling theory'. Outlined by American sociologist Howard Becker, labelling theory is premised on the idea that people's actions are judged and 'labelled' by the reactions of others. For example, if a mother mildly smacks her child on the backside in a public place, some passers-by may react with a disapproving sigh, but social reaction – and current laws – would judge this to be an acceptable act of chastisement. However, if the mother repeatedly slaps her child in the face, social reaction would label this sort of behaviour as abnormal and unacceptable – and the mother would no doubt find herself in serious trouble with the authorities.

This may seem like an extreme example, but labels are placed on individuals and groups by the rest of us in response to all sorts of actions and behaviour. The boundaries between normal and deviant, lawful and criminal, good and evil are established by this kind of 'social consensus' view. But in practice, social consensus is not entirely democratic. Some individuals and institutions within any society have greater power than others to react to situations, voice their opinions and attach labels to others. Politicians, magistrates, senior police officers, bishops, head-teachers and 'spokespeople' of various kinds are just some of those given the privileged position of shaping social reaction to a particular event or problem.

In today's world the media are, without doubt, the most central cog in this labelling process. Newspapers, for instance, don't just report on events of public interest; they endlessly comment on these events in a way that purports to reflect the public mood for days and weeks to come. The term 'viewspaper' – a recent addition to the English vernacular – refers to a growing trend for newspapers that place more emphasis on journalistic commentary than reportage. But 'viewspapers' aside, live rolling news on TV and radio requires a whole host of commentators to fill the air-time between the reporting of actual events. And even news media not interested in views and opinions need to tell the story of an event in a way that captivates audiences. So storytelling, too, effectively helps to construct wider social reaction to an event by drawing – if not downright labelling – the lines between good and bad, the acceptable and the unacceptable, the public interest or otherwise.

This may seem like another case of power inequality – not unlike problems of representation, political economy or information/ surveillance society – but labelling theory doesn't only account for the labelling power of the media. Labelling is a process that we all partake in – labels are not invented by the media, even though they certainly influence them. Moreover, when the lines between normal and deviant are clearly drawn, the labelling process can have a spiralling effect in further alienating those already labelled. This is known as 'deviance amplification'. Alienated individuals like, say, asylum seekers or drug dealers may turn to more deviant or criminal acts as the heat is turned on them by the rest of 'normal' society. To make matters worse, social reaction grows more hostile and harsher punitive measures are recommended to solve 'the rising problem', not least via the media.

But rather than surrender to deviance amplification, disaffected groups may begin to play up to their deviant image and label themselves in accordance with the unfavourable labels given to them by outsiders. The media, especially, provide a public platform through which deviant groups can show off the labels given to them by the rest of society. Moreover, labels can be created discretely from within deviant groups so as to prevent censure from outside. For example, drug dealers and their clientele use different terms to label different drugs (e.g. heroin is called junk, skag, civa, black tar, muck, pigment, etc). So labelling can occur from the outside and the inside. The role of the media in reinforcing 'outside' labels and revealing 'inside' ones is, of course, crucial.

THE MANUFACTURE OF NEWS

If news is all about telling stories, how do these stories get produced and what are their consequences for society? It's common knowledge that certain news sources tend to sensation-alise events with bold headlines and scathing commentary (the tabloid press being the main culprits in this respect). But a broader theory of news production, known as the 'manufacture-of-news' perspective, doesn't blame tabloid sensationalism alone. According to this perspective, news is always artificially constructed out of bits of reality, even when it claims to present events through the lens of objectivity. The fact is that news is a commodity to be bought and sold. The number-one quality of news, therefore, is its sales appeal. Reality is often just too damn dull! The news must sell, so reality must be carefully manufactured, packaged and fitted for purpose.

News is also perishable and must be made fresh daily. Just like bottles of milk, newspapers are delivered to people's front doors every morning – and are then recycled for future use (or used to wrap up fish and chips). You get 'slow news days' and 'not much news days', but you never get 'no news days' – oh no, that would see profits tumble and the whole news industry on its knees (now that would be news!). In summary, news is an FMCG (fast-moving consumer good) in need of constant reproduction for the sake of the reader/viewer/listener. If there's really no news, new news must be found, bottled up and manufactured. To invert that famous idiom, no news is bad news for news organisations.

Another idiom associated with the news media is that of the Fourth Estate. Historically, the First Estate belonged to the clergy; the Second Estate to royalty and aristocracy; and the Third Estate to the common masses of people (and their elected representa-tives in the democratic sense of the term). The Fourth Estate of the news press evolved as a significant feature of Western societies during the eighteenth and nineteenth centuries. However, statements about journalists being agents of democracy, upholders of honesty and integrity, investigative watchdogs, freedom-fighters and so on are somewhat farfetched and romantic notions, only true today of journalists forced to fight government controls and censorship. According to the manufacture-of-news perspective, while the media may function as the Fourth Estate in some countries, in many other contexts the media work against the public interests they claim to represent.

In the case of moral panics, news is manufactured for maximum impact. While the news media may not ignite the panic, they sure do stoke up the fire. Newsworthiness is all that really matters. News values typically include drama, spectacle, personality, brevity and topicality. Teenage gang violence is a no-brainer for the news reporter. Gang leaders and members must be found for 'on-the-spot' interviews, knives and guns must be shown in close-up (even if they bear no relation to actual events), action must be dramatically reconstructed, and the topical importance of the story must be blown out of all proportion by linking together totally unconnected sequences of violent events. Moreover, the 2003 Anti-Social Behaviour Order (ASBO) has allowed the British media to 'name and shame' anti-social children as well as adults. Ten-year-old kids are held up for public flogging. This may seem a little unfair – but it sure sells news and keeps the advertisers smiling.

But the journalists themselves are not really to blame for their news-manufacturing ways. After all, journalists can only work on the press releases given to them by the police, the courts, political parties and so on. Journalists are also constrained by the structures of their organisations and work practices. They must meet and beat tight deadlines, pursue leads, make decisions on the advice of editors, keep to certain routines and conventions, follow ethical codes, engage with colleagues on various tasks, make cups of tea and so on. To ease the pressures of time and space, news organisations often work with a 'diary' of news events. As Boorstin argues in relation to pseudo-events, most of the 'live' news we receive on TV and radio is planted, pre-planned and fully expected. Only rarely do events occur that are unexpected and entirely spontaneous. Partly because so much news production is not really new or revealing, in the rare event that news does emerge 'from nowhere' it is likely to provoke an unusually strong social reaction ('oh my God, this is really happening!'), which in turn lights the spark for its perpetual manufacture.

MORAL PANIC THEORY

In the seminal *Folk Devils and Moral Panics* (1972), South African sociologist Stan Cohen adapted labelling theory and the deviance-amplification model to the study of what he called 'moral panics'. His subject matter was social reaction to two competing youth subcultures in mid-1960s Britain – the mods and rockers. In a moral panic, Cohen states, 'a condition, episode, person or group of persons emerges to become defined as a threat to societal values and interests; its nature is presented in a stylised and stereotypical fashion by the mass media.'[18] So a problem is identified, the media report on this problem by representing and making free use of stereotypes (heroes versus villains, etc), social reaction follows, and the final nail in the coffin is the introduction of social controls (new laws, tougher policing, etc). Cohen showed how the moral panic provoked by the skirmishes between mods and rockers on the beaches of southern England labelled the perpetrators of this violence as 'folk devils': 'visible reminders of what we should not be.'[19] Folk devils are the personifications of moral panics, labelled as villains by 'right-thinking people' as well as the police and legal system, but hailed as martyrs by fellow outsiders.

Akin to the manufacture-of-news perspective, Cohen's moral-panic theory is grounded in the idea that the media did not merely *report*, in an objective way, the crowd disturbances between the mods and rockers. Far more crucially, the media actually helped to *construct* social reaction to the 'deviance' of the mods and rockers by sensationalising the level of violence and disruption. Tabloid newspapers, in particular, used dramatic phrases like 'screaming mob' and 'orgy of destruction'. These dramatic news reports led to increased concern about the threat posed by the mods and rockers to the rules and norms of mainstream society. The media also exaggerated the differences between the two youth subcultures – after all, the mods and rockers lived in the same working-class neighbourhoods. But subsequent media representations juxtaposing the mod subculture (scooters, the smart-casual image, the Beatles and Kinks motifs) against the rocker subculture (motorbikes, the Hell's Angels image, the Rolling Stones and Elvis motifs) cut deeper into differences and indirectly stirred up more conflict.

Moral-panic theory still strikes a chord in the relationship between the media and social fears today. And yet Cohen's ideas have not gone unchallenged. Some commentators argue that, while the media at the time undoubtedly aggravated the moral panic surrounding the mods and rockers, the wider historical context in which these two groups emerged clearly had a vital bearing on the hostile social reaction too. The affluent teenager of 1950s and 1960s Britain was a relatively new phenomenon, much disliked and distrusted by older generations less familiar with prosperity and spending power. Regardless of the media-fuelled moral panic, it may simply have been the case that the mods and rockers brought this pent-up generational tension (known as 'the generation gap') to a head. Moral-panic theory may also be guilty of overstating the spiralling effect of media coverage on the public-opinion dimension of social reaction. It is not uncommon for ordinary folk to attack the media for whipping up a frenzy about relatively trivial events of little public interest or consequence at all. Trial by media may appear rife – but most rational-thinking people prefer trial by jury, thank you very much.

SUBCULTURES

Youth subcultures like the mods and rockers clearly inspired moral-panic theory, but subcultural theory has a tradition of its own. Other examples of subcultures include the teds, punks, skinheads (or skins) and goths. Subcultures set themselves apart from the rest of society, opposing mainstream politics, religion, commerce and mass media. Yes, they are deviant, but their deviance is not primarily defined by the rest of society – subcultures actively choose to rebel against norms and conventions. Members of subcultures tend to be young, working class and alienated. Their radical values, motifs and actions aim to change the world around them, though at the same time they wish to remain underground, uncontaminated by consumer capitalism. Moral panics are therefore unhelpful distractions for subcultures in their attempts to resist incorporation into mainstream culture.

The most influential version of subcultural theory is British cultural critic Dick Hebdige's *Subculture* (1979). Two concepts underpin Hebdige's account: homology and *bricolage*. Homology is defined as the symbolic fit between the values of a subculture and the cultural products it uses to express these values. Music is one of the most essential media products used by homologous subcultures to express what they believe, fitting seamlessly alongside their choices of drugs, clothes, hairstyles and so on. Bands like The Sex Pistols in Britain and The Ramones in the United States expressed punks' homological opposition to societal rules and their anarchist spirit. Indeed, a moral panic was spread by the British tabloid press in 1976 when members of The Sex Pistols swore repeatedly on live TV.

Hebdige's other concept, *bricolage* (a French term for 'tinkering'), refers to the creative processes in which media and cultural products are invested with subcultural meanings that oppose their original functions. Punks practised *bricolage*, for instance, when they tinkered with dog collars and appropriated them as neckwear accessories – rather than use them on their pets. Digital music sampling – mixing and tinkering with previously released tracks – is a more recent case of rebellious *bricolage*. Taken together, homology and *bricolage* explain the power of subcultures to resist incorporation by the mainstream media and other powerful social forces, maintaining collective opposition to all things conformist, copyright and commercial.

Subcultures may well be regarded as beacons of resistance to the norm, moulding media products and cultural objects to fit their strong-minded beliefs and colourful styles, and rejecting the labels imposed upon them from above. Unfortunately, it is widely accepted by social commentators that genuine subcultures are dying out. Not since house music and rave culture of the late 1980s has there been a significant undercurrent of subcultural resistance, and it is even debatable whether rave was a unified subculture considering its mixed demographics and varied objectives. Rave and club cultures were also proactive in stirring up their own controversial publicity – a major departure from underground subcultures disassociating themselves from their moral-panic-ridden public image. Rave 'spokespeople', like editors of clubbing magazines, even appeared on TV news bulletins to argue their case for ecstasy being a recreational drug that could be consumed safely if users were educated properly. Such rampant courting of media attention was treated with deep suspicion by previous subcultures intent on protecting their subversive authenticity.

Another problem facing authentic subcultures is the speed and efficiency with which commercial operators gobble up their styles and values. No sooner are subcultures formed than they are marketed and popularised for the mass market. Chavs start buying into Burberry and 'bling' – and in a Chinese twinkle of an eye, a multi-million-dollar fashion and jewellery craze is set in operation. This situation alone would cloud the view that subcultures can effectively resist simultaneously the commercial exploitation and panicked reaction instigated by mainstream media culture. Perhaps *online* subcultures are the most authentic and viable forms of resistance today, bringing likeminded people across the world together to engage in illegal acts of piracy and file-sharing, among other subversive practices.

CENSORSHIP AND REGULATION

Censorship is the restriction and suppression of free speech. Regulation, on the other hand, attempts to set up control over what is said or shown without engaging in actual suppression. Moral panics fanned by political, religious and social commentators often result in media censorship and regulation, though in recent times exponents of 'freedom of the press' have won most of the arguments. For instance, several moves to block web content in Western countries have been revoked recently. In 2008, the German heavy-metal band Scorpions had the Wikipedia entry for their 1976 album *Virgin Killer* (depicting a naked, prepubescent girl on the sleeve cover) censored by the British-based Internet Watch Foundation (IWF). Only days later, after quite a lot of media debate, the IWF caved in to public pressure and relented. The campaign for freedom of speech, so popular among the libertarian movement that brought about the permissive society of the 1960s, has certainly matured to become an accepted feature of our social consensus.

Nonetheless, censorship of the media is a way of life in countries like China, Burma, Iran and North Korea. Chinese media are especially tightly censored, not least the internet. All Chinese websites require a government licence and all web content is carefully filtered by government officials. Many websites are blocked by the government and people's email inboxes are even subject to routine checks. The 'Great Firewall of China' also does its best to censor foreign websites containing information or entertainment deemed to be against the interests of the Chinese people. The government has even convinced major companies like Google and Yahoo to censor the results of Chinese versions of their search engines, with search terms like 'Tiananmen Square' strictly policed. Clearly due to the huge and largely untapped nature of the Chinese market, major media corporations are keen to stay on the right side of the state. After all, state-controlled capitalism is as good as any other type!

While censorship of mainstream media content is relatively rare in democracies like Britain and the United States, from time to time a film may be banned, a TV broadcaster suspended for infringing codes of conduct, a song's lyrics dubbed over and so on. Media regulation is more common but, like censorship, has been relaxed over recent decades. Indeed, during the 1980s the British TV industry was radically deregulated and privatised by the Thatcher government. Public service broadcasting became more market-driven. Reithian principles of education and moral decency traditionally associated with the BBC gave way to the demands of consumer sovereignty. Channel 4 became the new face of TV deregulation, commissioning content from independent production companies on competitive tenures rather than doing it in-house. In 1981, only three TV channels served the whole of Britain. Deregulation opened the door for the multichannel TV environment we encounter today. Ironically, a moral-panic backlash against deregulation and privatisation has been reflected in recent years by renewed fears about 'video nasties', hardcore pornography and ease of access to other violent or obscene content.

Censorship and regulation are typical responses to moral panics about media effects. For example, the cinema in Britain enjoyed scant censorship or regulation in its early years. Children and adults alike could choose to view any film that took their fancy. It was not until the 1910s, when a press-fuelled moral panic associated street crime with adolescents attending screenings of violent films, that age classifications were imposed on films. Famously, 1950s TV performances of Elvis Presley's gyrating hips were censored from the waist down.

In the twenty-first century, moral panics chiefly centred on video games and the internet have led to new forms of censorship. In each case, children and young people are seen as both the perpetrators and victims of anti-social behaviour – they become the excuse for politicians and policymakers to impose stricter laws and tighter regulations on new forms of media and popular culture. So once the honeymoon period is over, most media and cultural forms undergo some form of censorship or regulation. As new technologies replace old, the honeymoon-regulation-deregulation cycle continues. Opponents of censorship, on the other hand, go on campaigning for complete freedom of speech. Sometimes, in the face of unnecessary panic, anti-censorship campaigners are praised as 'voices of reason'. But on those (relatively rare) occasions when media-fuelled moral panics reflect the social consensus, campaigners are derided for their callously liberal outlooks and vegetarian sensibilities.

CELEBRITY AND FANDOM

From moral panics to celebrity and fandom – an appropriate move when we consider how words like 'hysteria', 'fanaticism', 'craze' and 'mania' cut through all three of these media-studies topics. Indeed, 'celebrity culture' has become a cliché to describe today's fascination with fame and the famous. But we should tread with caution. Celebrity is not a new phenomenon. Alexander the Great was a celebrity of ancient Greece thanks to his military prowess; William Shakespeare was a famous name in his day as well as ours; and in terms of sporting celebrity, nineteenth-century English cricketer William Gilbert (WG) Grace is widely regarded as the greatest player of all time. Being a fan is not a new experience either. The history of fandom has its roots in huge swathes of people trying to catch sight of their hero achieving some great feat of sporting or athletic achievement, like swimming across the English Channel or running the four-minute mile. Celebrity and fandom (and moral panics about both) have always gone hand in hand.

And yet these days it seems celebrities are not satisfied with just their fans – everyone gets bombarded with celebrity images. Several historical changes have brought celebrity to the forefront of contemporary media culture. Perhaps the most important change has been the declining role of religion in modern times. The only approved celebrities in sacred times were biblical figures, with God and Jesus Christ sitting quite high up in Christian people's estimations. Worshipping anyone or anything not connected to Christianity was denounced as the Devil's work. As time went by, monarchs replaced biblical figures with the divine rights of Kings and Queens – God's servants on Earth – forming the basis for their celebrity status. But once democratic governance had become a mainstay of developed countries, so powerful dictators and political leaders were resigned to the history books. New public figures, closer to what we would now call celebrities, began to enter the realm of politics and public affairs.

And a further key change was the turn to consumer capitalist culture in the early half of the twentieth century. Products needed consumers, so new roles were created for 'product ambassadors' to endorse and promote these consumables. At the same time, celebrities could be consumed on a routine basis too, in the music hall, at the cinema, in magazines and so on. And alongside the rise of consumerism, the growth of the mass media changed what it meant to be a celebrity – and threw a far greater number of famous people into the public eye than would otherwise have been possible. So what have celebrities got that the rest of us haven't?

CHARISMA

Individuals who achieve fame thanks to some special talent or gift are said to possess charisma. German sociologist Max Weber has a lot to say about charisma in relation to political leaders and their followers. Most political systems, Weber claims, operate as bureaucracies governed by rational structures like stock markets and constitutional laws. By contrast, charisma is a form of political leadership that achieves consensus without the need for bureaucratic structures. Weber views the charismatic individual as someone blessed with supernatural, god-like powers. Names like

Adolf Hitler and Winston Churchill are associated with charisma. It was their individual magnetism and charm, more so than the political regimes to which they belonged, that wooed the hearts and minds of their respective nations. However, Weber points out that charisma is not entirely self-generated – only when people unanimously direct their feelings and emotions towards an individual does he or she become adorned with charismatic powers.

The media celebrity, like the political leader, may also be adorned with charisma. The BBC radio comedian Tommy Handley, some have argued, was as much of a morale-booster to the British people in the Second World War as Churchill. And with the rise of TV, Muhammad Ali and Elvis Presley became as charismatic as any world leader has ever been. It may, in fact, be easier for celebrities to take risks with their charismatic personalities than political leaders who are, after all, publically accountable for their actions. So while charisma is a magical ingredient that enables certain individuals to chemically react with everyone else, it also requires a radical, carefree attitude on the part of the charismatic. It's no surprise to find that many charismatic figures over the course of history possessed lots of wealth before their true charisma shone through, so that holding down a job mattered not in the least, and saying and doing what one liked became routine.

But how do charismatic individuals captivate with such compelling force? The answer may reside in Freudian psychoanalysis. Freud claims that the mind works on three drives: the id, ego and superego. The id is the unconscious, irrational drive associated with wants, desires and instincts (young children exhibit this drive); the ego is the conscious drive equated with reason and socially acceptable behaviour; and the superego is the drive through which we acquire a moral conscience of what is right and wrong. For fully fledged adults, the ego and superego are the source of most day-to-day mental processes, whereas the id is filled with wishes and longings 'that shall not be named' and are suppressed by our consciousness (indeed, the id only reveals its dark side in our dreams). Following Freud, some psychoanalysts believe that the secret of charisma is its capacity to tap into people's ids and activate suppressed desires. This process occurs when people develop a strong identification with leaders or celebrities, treating them as father figures and themselves as id-ridden children. This would explain feelings of love, infatuation and immense pride that some people acquire for an individual only known to them via the media – and their outpourings of untold grief when a charismatic figure dies.

CELEBRITIES

So celebrities possess charisma, though some have more than others. But are celebrities all the same? The short answer is 'no' – and we've not discussed the difference between celebrity and stardom yet! According to British sociologist Chris Rojek's *Celebrity* (2001), there are three types:

1. Ascribed celebrity: this is predetermined celebrity status based on bloodlines, as with members of the royal family or sons and daughters of famous people. Prince William is an ascribed celebrity, as is Chelsea Clinton.
2. Achieved celebrity: this type is granted to individuals who accomplish greatness thanks to some special talent, skill or quality. Greats of the sporting world like Roger Federer and Venus Williams are achieved celebrities.
3. Attributed celebrity: in this case, individuals become celebrities without having any great talent or famous bloodline. Their celebrity is entirely media-generated, whether they like it or not. Reality-TV personalities like the late Jade Goody (former Big Brother contestant) are attributed celebrities, as are individuals forced into the media limelight due to tragic circumstances, like Kate and Gerry McCann.

Clearly, all three types of celebrity are prevalent today, and some individuals arguably fit into more than one type. For example, George W Bush is both an achieved celebrity (eight years as US President was something of an achievement) and an ascribed celebrity (his father, George H W Bush, also held the Presidency). It is the attributed-celebrity type, though, which is the most distinctive product of twenty-first-century media culture. Ordinary people are becoming celebrities like never before, changing the very meaning of the term (Boorstin and Warhol are proving truly prophetic). The media love transforming the ordinary into the extraordinary, because 'rags to riches' stories about people who may live next door to us are attention-grabbing – they sell newspapers, advertising space, phone-in votes and all the rest.

STARS

Stars may also become adorned with charisma. So what's the difference between a celebrity and a star? Celebrities, on the whole, appear as themselves across an array of different media. Tiger Woods is always Tiger Woods (even on a bad day!). Stars, however, take on meanings both in who they are and the characters they perform. Stars are, first and foremost, actors in search of characters. Tom Cruise is very often not Tom Cruise (even on a good day!). Tom Cruise being interviewed on a chat show is Tom Cruise the celebrity, but on film he is always acting out a character, and celebrity and character combine to generate the star persona that is 'Tom Cruise'.

These days we take stardom for granted – film stars, pop stars, reality-TV stars, stars in their eyes, *Dancing with the Stars* (2005–), Michelin-star-rated chefs, stars on the Hollywood Walk of Fame, star vehicles, five-stars and more stars. But the origins of stardom, in the American star system, have a chequered history. The major film studios were reluctant at first to promote the names of actors lest they benefited financially at the expense of other employees (cameramen, designers, lighting technicians, tea ladies, etc). But, by about 1915, once Hollywood had replaced the East Coast as the home of film production, the studios realised just how precious the star commodity could be. Stars began to promote movies and movie theatres – and soon they began promoting themselves.

At the same time, the first Hollywood stars, like Charlie Chaplin and Mary Pickford, got together and formed a company called United Artists to reflect their growing economic independence from the studios. By the 1950s and 1960s the tables had turned, with the star system helping to keep Hollywood afloat as the studios fell into decline. But it was not until the end of this period that the star system finally shrugged off industry constraints that had limited the range of personalities able to make the break into the big time. Until the late 1960s, for instance, there were only two types of male star: the tough guy (like John Wayne or James Dean) and the sophisticated gent (like Fred Astaire or Cary Grant).

In *Stars* (1979), British film theorist Richard Dyer analyses star charisma as an ideological construction. Dyer claims that 'star images function crucially in relation to contradictions within and between ideologies, which they seek variously to manage and resolve'.[20] But in exceptional circumstances, Dyer argues, stars embody oppositional roles in relation to dominant ideologies. For instance, Muhammad Ali (who may be defined as a celebrity and a star, given his role-playing character) refused to join the US army during the Vietnam War, and espoused Black Islamic beliefs at a time when 'White America' called the shots. Ali's guru at the time, black civil-rights activist Malcolm X, was another anti-conformist star.

Whether a star conforms to or opposes the dominant ideologies of their time is not the deciding factor in their star status, though. For Dyer, stars must resonate with people by capturing the ideological tensions of their time. He uses the example of

1950s Hollywood star Marilyn Monroe. Yes, she was beautiful; yes, she could sing and act; but these attributes alone were not sufficient for her to achieve greatness. After all, there are lots of beautiful actors out there, but not all of them become stars. What Monroe possessed, according to Dyer, was a contradictory blend of virginal innocence and sexual voluptuousness that resonated both with traditionalist views on women and beauty, as well as more liberal, feminist ideologies about permissive sexuality and freedom of speech. Monroe became a star because she personified and encompassed the competing social values of her adoring public.

Stars certainly are a complex breed. A select few play more or less the same role every time (Arnold Schwarzenegger is the archetypal action hero), but as the star system has gained in sophistication over the years, so the need for stars to play authentic, versatile roles – and avoid typecasting – has become more pressing. Dyer suggests three ways in which a star's image is constructed for the sake of authenticity and versatility:

1. Selective use: this is the process of revealing certain aspects of a star's image and concealing others, through the use of lighting, scripting, costume and so on. Renee Zellweger, for example, was selectively made to look like a plain, plump thirty-something in *Bridget Jones's Diary* (2001), but has since gone on to appear in films playing glamorously beautiful – and wafer-thin – roles.

2. Perfect fit: in this case, the star's image and their character become indistinguishable. So Jim Carrey as slapstick comedian and impersonator in the Ace Ventura films or *Bruce Almighty* (2003) amounts to a perfect fit.

3. Problematic fit: this occurs when the star and their character contradict each other. Sometimes the problem is miscasting, but if the problematic fit is resolved successfully, the star may receive wide acclaim for rediscovering their ideal image. John Travolta's hitman role in *Pulp Fiction* (1994) was a problematic fit that helped to trans-

form his career – and finally rid him of the typecast image he constructed in *Grease* (1978) and *Saturday Night Fever* (1977).

These days, in particular, even if they usually seek roles that provide the perfect fit, the most popular and long-lasting stars – those who resonate with our times and appear to be the most authentic – partake in all three of these image constructions.

PARA-SOCIAL INTERACTION

Another way of understanding stars and celebrities is to think about how they interact with their public. Analogous to ordinary social interaction of the face-to-face kind, para-social interaction refers to the *apparent* familiarity between media personalities and audiences. This familiarity may become a substitute for more traditional sources of familiarity like interactions between relatives and friends. Para-social interaction can be fostered through intimate media performances. For instance, the conversational style of radio and TV close-ups of individual performers help to nurture personal attachments in listeners and viewers. Studio audiences also play an important function in coaching wider social attitudes. So a studio audience cues the media audience on when to laugh, cheer, cry, gasp with horror and so on.

In their seminal essay 'Mass Communication and Para-Social Interaction' (1956), American media theorists Donald Horton and R Richard Wohl discuss the concept of 'personae' as well as para-social interaction. Personae are the celebrity personalities who build up intimate, para-social relations with media audiences. What matters is that personae provide 'a continuing relationship' for audiences and that their characters remain unchanged in a world of otherwise distressing change. So para-social interactions with personae give people means to escape from the uncertainties endemic in their real interactions with one another. But Horton and

Wohl show that personae must work hard in order to receive wide-spread affection. Expert presentations of self are the stimulus for para-social intimacy – the omnipresence of the media is not enough to guarantee celebrity-audience familiarity. Therefore, personae deploy tricks of the trade – mingling with studio audiences, mixing sincerity with comedy, breaking into song – to effectively invite para-social relationships with individuals who they cannot see or hear or know anything about.

A similar but more contemporary version of para-social interaction is British sociologist John Thompson's notion of 'mediated quasi-interaction' (in *The Media and Modernity*, 1995). He uses the term 'quasi-interaction' (resembling interaction) because the kind of interaction between media personalities and audiences is not immediately reciprocal; not completely interactive. Email or face-to-face conversations allow for reciprocity, but interactions between, say, TV celebrities and their viewing public allow no scope for instantaneous exchanges of opinion. To a large degree, the TV celebrity determines the rules of exchange. They possess what Thompson calls 'televisibility' – a contradictory mix of spatial-temporal distance and audio-visual presence. In other words, they are located outside the space and time occupied by audiences, but they are strangely present to our eyes and ears all the same. This explains the odd feelings we experience when we actually do come face-to-face with a famous media personality. The yawning gap between a celebrity's 'televisible' presence and their momentary co-presence in our lives often takes us by surprise ('I didn't realise she was so short', 'He was picking his nose', etc) and shatters the illusion carefully manufactured in mediated quasi-interactions.

Mediated quasi-interaction and 'televisibility' are not just thrown into confusion by occasional face-to-face encounters, either. The other half of the quasi-interaction (i.e. the media audience) bears down upon the 'televisible' relationship too. Celebrities being interviewed by TV news presenters, for example, must be careful not to 'lose their cool' or say anything too controversial for fear of audience disaffection. Of course, media personalities of all kinds undergo rigorous PR training that aims to maximise their saleability and minimise 'bad press'. Politicians go further in using spin doctors to advise them on which sound-bites to voice (and avoid) before they expose themselves to the potential pitfalls of, say, a presidential TV debate.

But regardless of PR training and spin-doctoring, Thompson shows how the media provide a platform for the all-seeing public eye, forcing celebrities to be accountable for their words and actions. Media audiences, in turn, act upon what they see and hear in mediated quasi-interactions for mostly democratic, positive ends. It is often the case, for example, that the public are more favourable to honest people who they can 'connect with' – even if these 'honest people' are multimillionaire celebrities with rather messy private lives. In comparison, celebrities who lie about their private lives, or say one thing and do another, are condemned as hypocrites, and soon lose their fans and followers. Put simply, parasocial and mediated quasi-interaction alike can make or break celebrity status.

FANS

So although initiated by celebrities and media performers of one sort or another, para-social and mediated quasi-interaction need audiences to complete the communication circle. An important media studies approach to audiences focuses on the role of fans. The term 'fan' is short for 'fanatic'. Fanatics are usually viewed with disapproval. They are obsessed, crazy, just plain silly about whatever it is they invest their time and energy in. But fans are also vital commodities for media industries and, by extension, the careers of celebrities. Fans help celebrities to secure lucrative sponsorship deals and help the media to sell advertising space, among other things. In fact, the importance of a celebrity (A-list, B-list, etc) is easily measured by the size of their fan club. Audiences come and go, but fans are loyal consumers who buy not just the magazines or CDs or DVDs, but the mugs, t-shirts, fashion accessories, hair products, biographies, pin-up posters, concert tickets, subscriptions, football boots, golf clubs, limited-edition box-sets... ad infinitum.

So are fans just plain silly? The 'yes' argument sees fans as successfully targeted media consumers of what the major corporations choose to distribute and promote to them. Adorno's culture-industry perspective rendered fans of pop music as 'emotional types' seduced by the phony individuality of their cynically manufactured idols. The perennial figure of the 'teenybopper' girl fan is a case in point. The music industry has traditionally constructed a binary model of fandom in which boys are targeted by the marketing ploys used to promote male rock bands, while girls are targeted by campaigns surrounding easy-listening heartthrobs and divas. This state of affairs (until recently) has been manifested in the fact that very few female rock musicians have enjoyed anything other than fleeting careers, the common perception being that rock chicks cater for neither male nor female fans. The long-established success of the music industry in digging this gender divide for its own promotional purposes doesn't bode well for the progressive view of fandom as consumer empowerment.

On the other hand, some celebrities do very well by developing a fan base that transcends girl/boy, pop/rock divisions. Madonna, for example, has changed her persona throughout her long and successful career – including her gender image and sexual identity – thus helping her to hone a loyal and complex fan base (male, female, straight, gay, bisexual and so on). The aforementioned consumer-power theorist Fiske asserts that 'the teenage-girl fan of Madonna who fantasises her own empowerment can translate this fantasy into behaviour, and can act in an empowered way socially, thus winning more social territory for herself'.[21] So Madonna is a role model for young female fans in the way she deals with taboo subjects like lesbianism in playful and progressive ways. Madonna is the villain of patriarchy and the hero of feminist identity politics. Quite simply, Fiske claims that fans of celebrities who try to break away from standardised formulae for success achieve equally progressive ends in their own lives.

Fiske's theory of consumer resistance, though highly contestable, has inspired subsequent media ethnographies of fan cultures. The best of these, *Textual Poachers* (1992), by American literary theorist Henry Jenkins, strongly defends fan practices as meaningful, creative and productive. Jenkins argues that 'fans actively assert their mastery over the mass-produced texts which provide the raw materials for their own cultural productions and the basis for their social interactions'.[22] Fans are not led – like a dog on a lead – to decode dominant, negotiated or oppositional codes in the media they consume. On the contrary, Jenkins sees fans as ordinary people who, at particular moments in their lives, engage in extraordinarily committed activities that go way beyond the bounds of even the most cunning producer's or publicist's imagination.

Moreover, Jenkins argues that fans can affect the kinds of decisions made in the media production process. Fans often try to interact, not just with themselves, but with media producers and celebrities in order to express their own views, for instance, on what the sleeve design should look like for a band's latest album. Fans also encode their own fan texts (fanzines, webzines and so on) and attend conventions, conferences and other social events. Trekkies – the name given to an international network of fans of American TV serial *Star Trek* (1966–9) – are perhaps the best example of what Jenkins calls the 'participatory culture' of media-generated fandom. A more recent example of fan participation was provoked by cult teen TV drama *The OC* (2003–7), which generated a string of fan websites and forums dedicated to the show and its central characters. Fans are not passive consumers who need to 'get a life'; they are active donors for the lifeblood of their favourite media and celebrity texts. And fan artists – individuals who create and sometimes sell artwork devoted to their favourite things – are participants par excellence.

The roots of the two-sided debate about the merits or demerits of fandom are astutely revealed by Ang in her study of American TV serial *Dallas* (previously discussed vis-à-vis political economy). Those of Ang's respondents who disliked *Dallas* could comfortably adopt a critical stance from within the ideology of mass culture in their argument that it was a cynical appeasement of American cultural values. However, *Dallas* fans were without a similarly powerful ideological framework when trying to explain their pleasure in watching the serial. Ang suggests that these fans could only articulate an ideology of populism – 'no one can account for taste' – which was demeaned for pandering to the language of consumerism. Effectively, fans were left without a powerful ideological consumer position because they had no overriding perception of any ideological function in the product they consumed. In summary, it is harder to formulate a reasoned argument to justify feelings over thoughts, than thoughts over feelings. This proves the point that fan pleasure is too easily derided as irrational, and that critics of fans are no less emotive – and not necessarily more convincing – in their value judgements than fans themselves.

NARRATIVE AND GENRE

Like celebrity and stardom, narrative and genre are highly constructed and manufactured – even when they appear not to be. In the same way that stars are marketed to sell films or popular music, so narrative styles and generic categories are clearly drawn to encourage audiences to identify with the type of film or music being pitched at them. Ambiguity is a recipe for disaster in the fiercely competitive realm of commercial media. But narrative and genre (also like celebrity) depend on audiences as much as producers. Audiences must 'get' the narrative and be able to 'place' the genre – and if they do and they can (and if they like what they see, read or hear), then communities of fans and followers will emerge to bring longevity to the media products in question. Therefore, the media use narrative and genre conventions to foster familiarity and stoke the embers of popular appeal. And probably the best-known media convention comes packaged in six little words.

WHO, WHAT, HOW, WHERE, WHEN, WHY

English poet Rudyard Kipling may well be the originator of this classic news formula. In *The Elephant's Child* (1902), he wrote:

I keep six honest serving men:
(They taught me all I knew)
Their names are What and Where and When
And How and Why and Who.

Journalists have followed this simple narrative model since time immemorial, though it can be applied to narratives other than just the news. Sporting contests, feature films, documentaries, song lyrics and all kinds of other media narratives follow this same formula. The 'who', the 'what', the 'how', the 'where', the 'when' and the 'why' are demanded by readers and audiences in order to sustain their interest. In fact, the answers to these six questions construct the framework for our everyday conversations with friends and acquaintances. It is the 'when' question, though, that is often the most pressing for journalists and storytellers. Narratives about events that have only just unfolded – or, even better, are still unfolding – afford newer and more dramatic details than narratives from the depths of history. On the other hand, the 'why' question is often the most mooted and the least frequently answered. Some narratives (especially true ones) are too difficult and would take too long to explain. This is the basis for the common-felt concern about how the news media spend more time entertaining their audiences than educating them.

Another formula familiar to journalists is known as the 'inverted pyramid'. Like an upside-down pyramid, news narratives provide details in descending order of newsworthiness, with the most substantial information contained at the top. So the opening paragraph of a newspaper report or the 'lead-in' to a TV news item will provide almost everything that the reader or viewer needs to know. The rest of the narrative will then add 'flesh to the bones' by reporting on events in more depth. This formula caters especially for tabloid consumers without the time or inclination to read or watch long and complicated news narratives. Most of us lead hectic lives and the news must fit into our busy schedules, otherwise we put the newspaper down or switch to another TV channel. Journalists and sub-editors know this, so they cut stories from the bottom up. If the first sentence of a report or the opening seconds of a bulletin are punchy enough to grab our attention, then we will read on and venture 'down the pyramid'. Otherwise, we keep on browsing for something that does grab us. If nothing grabs us, the whole narrative ceases to operate – no narrative ever survives without an author *and* an audience.

CLASSIC REALISM

The point about news-narrative formulae is that they seek to reconstruct events in the most accurate, informative and compelling ways. This is precisely what the classic-realist narrative does too. The term 'classic realism' is associated primarily with the nineteenth-century novel. English novelists Charles Dickens and Thomas Hardy, for example, are generally regarded as classic-realist novelists. Their novels try to represent the reality of London and Wessex life respectively. The omniscient narrator is central to this reconstruction of objective reality. Omniscient narrators play God, looking down on characters and events with an all-seeing eye. Likewise, the reader is party to all the knowledge and power that the omniscient narrator enjoys. First-person narratives are conspicuous by their absence. Subjectivity and multiple-character perspectives are strictly forbidden. Classic realism represents reality with the guidance of a unified, continuous and ever-present narrative voice.

But the classic-realist narrative doesn't stop at novels. Most of our media today aim at realism to some degree, regardless of postmodernist claims that realism and reality are lost forever. This explains why computer and video games are so reviled for the shockingly realistic ways in which they construct narratives that place gamers in control of their destinies. TV dramas, including soaps, share realist narrative conventions too. Viewers are positioned as invisible onlookers with the perfect vantage point from which to follow the narrative, wherever and whenever it goes. And British film theorist Colin MacCabe associates classic-realist novels with classic Hollywood film style. In 'Realism and the Cinema' (1974), MacCabe points to the seamless camera action that 'shows things the way they are' and conceals the 'constructedness' of the film narrative. Continuity editing and linear narrative conventions, for instance, hide the artificial processes that go into filmmaking and help to create objective, omniscient narration akin to a Dickens or Hardy novel. Of course, non-realist narratives (e.g. surrealist or science-fiction narratives) occur in films and other media too, but they are a small blob on the realist-dominated narrative landscape through which we daily travel.

NARRATIVE THEORY

There are two main types of media narrative: 'open' and 'closed'. Open narratives are continuous and have no certain ending. TV soaps and drama serials are open narratives – and remain so until the curtain comes down due to poor ratings or departures of key personnel. Likewise, some news stories remain open and without immediate resolution, as in 'The case continues...' convention of court reporting. The other type, closed narratives, have a clear beginning, middle and end, like most films and pop songs. Whether a narrative is opened or closed determines a number of outcomes. Open narratives must accommodate new as well as existing audiences, so characters and action need to refer back to previous narrative developments. In comparison, closed narratives presuppose a constant audience from start to finish. Another difference between the two narrative styles relates to characterisation. Open narratives allow characters to move in and out of different status roles quite fluidly. One week a soap character may suffer ill fortune and be pitied, whereas the next week their luck changes and they climb back up the social ladder. In a closed film narrative, by contrast, characters are less likely to change status (except, perhaps, towards the end) and a hierarchy is usually maintained.

Every narrative is different from the next one. It is even accepted wisdom to treat, say, a novel and the film version of that novel (and the screenplay) as separate narratives. Nonetheless, two prominent narrative theorists have identified similar features common to all stories, regardless of their media or cultural properties. Russian folklorist Vladimir Propp examined the functions of characters in hundreds of old folktales. He was not interested in the characters themselves but in their actions, and the ways in which these actions helped to progress the narrative. In *Morphology of the Folk Tale* (1928), Propp identifies eight character roles serving narrative functions:

1. The villain, who creates the narrative complication.
2. The hero, who seeks something and ultimately returns, with the complication resolved and the villain defeated.
3. The donor, who supports the hero (often providing them with magic).
4. The helper, a companion to the hero.
5. The princess, who is the victim of the villain until the hero saves her (and then gets to keep her, with the marriage thrown in).
6. The father, who rewards the hero (with the princess among other things).
7. The dispatcher, who tells the hero about his task (and when to return).
8. The false hero, who appears to be good but turns out to be bad (or, at least, not as good as the real hero).

Propp's narrative functions have been used to analyse a whole variety of media narratives. Generally speaking, the more fantasy-fictional the narrative, the more these character roles will apply. So they appear in *The Wizard of Oz* (1939), the *Star Wars* and Bond movies, for example; but in film and media narratives without obvious goodies and baddies, these functions are not so evident. The princess and father roles are somewhat outdated, for sure, though the other six roles still conjure up plenty of examples.

Another prominent narrative theory is to be found in the concept of 'equilibrium' discussed by Bulgarian literary theorist Tzvetan Todorov in *The Poetics of Prose* (1971). According to Todorov, most narratives begin with a state of equilibrium, where people and events are assumed to be in the same, routine state as they were before the narrative began. There then follows – often quite soon into the narrative – a problem that brings about disruption. Recognition of the disruption then ensues, followed by attempts to overcome this disruption. Finally, the disruption is remedied and a state of equilibrium returns as the narrative ends.

This may seem like another case of epic, heroic narrative structure, but the disruption may be relatively trivial and the return to equilibrium straightforward. For example, the weather forecast may present a narrative about stormy weather, and we overcome such a disruption by deciding not to climb a mountain, so returning us to the warmth and happiness of our homes. Todorov's equilibrium model can be applied, in fact, to almost any closed narrative. But its universality also draws attention to its limitations – it is so simple that it turns out to be simplistic and tells us little about the specific qualities that go into narrative making. So let's leave our discussion of narrative perpetually unresolved and wander down another theoretical avenue.

GENRE THEORY

What is a genre? This question needs addressing because genres, sub-genres and meta-genres are everywhere in the media. The term 'genre' was first applied to films, but has since spread to music, radio, TV, books, magazines and more. Put simply, a genre is a body of individual products that share certain things in common. So genre theory assumes that media and cultural productions work in groups or categories to generate collective meanings. The argument goes that one horror film unfolds much like another, one pop ballad is structured like another, one sitcom contains the same jokes as another – even if there are always certain differences (however minimal) to distinguish between like products. As British film scholar Stephen Neale points out in *Genre* (1980), 'Genres are not to be seen as forms of textual codifications, but as systems of orientations, expectations and conventions that circulate between industry, text and subject.'[23] As such, genre theory flies in the face of conventional wisdom in literary and film theory – particularly *auteur* theory – which studies singular texts (poems, novels, films, etc) in isolation and evaluates them in terms of their uniqueness or originality. On the contrary, genre theory is only concerned with the interconnectedness between texts.

So who or what creates genres? This is a moot point because genre theory effectively writes off individual authors, directors, artists, producers and anyone else who may lay claim to authority or copyright. The Beatles may be the greatest guitar-rock band of all time, but they didn't invent the rock genre and their rock music is not the only type ever produced. Clearly some artists and producers have had more influence than others in the making of a genre, but it is rare for an individual (or even a small group) to become universally recognised as that genre's *raison d'être*. It is fair to say, too, that genres are not necessarily created at the point of production. The whole post-production packaging and marketing campaign helps to complement the production content by placing a product within familiar, pre-existing generic parameters. For example, the sleeve design of a heavy-metal album often draws on previous design conventions within that genre (blood, skulls, snakes and daggers feature quite a lot) and is in stark contrast to the sleeve design of, say, the latest manufactured pop act.

But genres are not just the work of producers and marketing people. Genres are also created by those consumers who buy into them. Think of 'broadsheet readers' or 'rom-com lovers' or 'quiz-show addicts'. Often genre labels directly map onto consumer types. But now we get into that difficult chicken-and-egg debate. Which came first in the creation of a genre – marketing 'spin' or audience demand? For the sake of diplomacy, most media theorists see genre as an even split between marketing and audience influences; production and consumption processes. Like the construction of celebrity and stardom, genres are dynamic categories forever undergoing changes in their meanings and popularity. The Western film genre, for example, was hugely popular for a previous generation of producers and consumers, but today's filmmakers and filmgoers are not so inclined. One way of getting around this problem is to spoof the Western genre, along the lines of *Wild Wild West* (1999). But a serious Western is unlikely to satisfy contemporary filmic tastes and trends. This brings us to another debate about the continuing relevance of genre categories in a mixed-up world full of competing influences and shifting sensibilities.

COMMUNITIES AND SCENES

Genres that clearly emerge out of common interests among producers and consumers are said to form 'genre communities'. Country music followers and practitioners, say, belong to a community. They may not all live in the same places (though many come from the country!), but they regularly get together, in both the interpersonal and mediated sense, to share their love for Shania Twain, Garth Brooks and other non-commercial country musicians. Other genre communities meet at rock festivals, film festivals, art-cinema screenings, gaming conferences, book clubs and so on. The point is that there is a clearly identifiable cultural heritage around which artists, producers, musicians, audiences, readers, roadies, collectors, dealers and others congregate. Where a community is strong and where the boundaries between insiders and outsiders are clear-cut, the associative genre will live on in good health.

But genre communities are rarely fixed and sealed from external pressures and internal conflicts, and when fractures appear within these communities, the demise of the genre is inevitable too. An alternative way of understanding genre, emerging from popular music studies, is the notion of 'scene'. A scene exists where a range of musical tastes and practices come together like a jigsaw puzzle. Music scenes are less stable than genre communities because they attempt to accommodate differences. Whereas communities are sociologically measurable (the kinds of people who belong to them share similar demographic characteristics), scenes are less tangible and far more diverse in character.

The shift from genre communities to scenes is a combined outcome of more eclectic consumer behaviour and subsequent changes in global music-industry trends. 1980s stadium rock (Bruce Springsteen, U2, Dire Straits) and the genre communities it spawned have been superseded by the rise of more localised music scenes revolving around electronic dance music. Indeed, the term 'dance music' only really describes a meta-genre (or meta-scene) of various smaller scenes – house, garage, hip hop, trance, techno, R n B and so on – not to mention the local nuances (or sub-genres) within each of these scenes (house breaks down into acid house, old skool Chicago house, Italian house, new skool house and so on). So a scene is a complex fusion of global and local influences that doesn't follow a particular genre tradition, but instead embraces a range of genres, sub-genres and localised narratives in its systems of production and consumption. This explains why dance-music scenes favour compilations of tracks featuring a range of artists from across the world, whereas mono-generic discographies of bands' albums remain the preserve of rock communities.

NEW MEDIA

Twentieth-century media have largely followed a broadcasting model of general-interest information and entertainment for a mass audience (national or international). What we might now call 'old media' communicated their messages via analogue signals. Analogue TV and radio signals, for example, encoded picture and sound information (recorded in production) and transmitted it via continuously variable frequency waves to aerials on the roofs of people's homes – or antenna attached to the receiving sets. Although analogue signals allow for two-way communication – early radio devices could operate as receivers and transmitters – the prospect of millions of two-way radio circuits jamming up limited frequency-wave capacity was clearly unworkable.

Yet as twenty-first-century digital media have come to replace the old, opportunities for interactivity between producers and consumers have multiplied. Digital signals are not continuous signals of varying frequency but work rather like switches that turn on or off. This binary code of positive and non-positive states is represented by two digits, 'one' and 'zero'. More complicated sequences of codes involving more digits are possible but awkward to engineer in practice, so the binary code is considered the most robust in storing and transmitting data effectively (although digital signals are subject to external interference much like analogue ones). Digital media like mobile phones, digital cameras, internet applications, MP3 music players, DAB radios and digital TV are what the term 'new media' refers to. New media are inextricably linked with digital computer technology, in particular. Some commentators even talk of a 'Digital Revolution' that has occurred since the last decade of the twentieth century. But critics of the idea suggest that contemporary media change has been more evolutionary than revolutionary. The printing press and the electric telegraph, yes, but has the internet really transformed our lives? Let's consider some critical and contestable concepts before we wallow in careless clichés.

CONVERGENCE

Convergence has several meanings in media studies. In the context of media economics and ownership, it means large-scale vertical integration in which different industries (production, distribution, advertising, etc) converge together under the umbrella of a major media conglomerate like Time Warner. But economic convergence is certainly not peculiar to new media. In fact, new-media ownership mirrors patterns of ownership and control in traditional media sectors like TV and film. Just five corporations, for example, dominate the broadband internet market in the UK: British Telecom, Telefonica Europe (O2), News Corporation (Sky), Time Warner (AOL) and Virgin Media.

Ownership of the most popular websites has increasingly fallen into the hands of major corporations too. Flickr is owned by Yahoo and News Corporation owns MySpace. Facebook turned down a $1 billion offer from Yahoo in 2007 – while, in the same year, Microsoft bought a minority stake in the social networking site for $240 million, valuing Facebook at $15 billion (not surprising, given its huge pull in terms of advertising revenue). And Yahoo itself was the target of an unsuccessful $44.6 billion bid by Microsoft in 2008. A decade of Google, meanwhile, has been a story of success after success. It's now the most powerful internet corporation by some distance, as evidenced by its acquisition of YouTube for $1.65 billion in 2006 and the even more lucrative $3.1 billion takeover of online advertising competitor DoubleClick the following year. Google has expanded its advertising activities to other media sectors such as TV and mobile phones too. So in political-economy terms, there is nothing new about new-media convergence – it's the same old merry-go-round of takeovers, mergers, substantial shareholdings and diversification.

But in technological terms, convergence means the coming together of different media through digital technologies. The terms 'convergence' and 'multimedia' are more or less synonymous. Both terms capture how computer-chip technology has taken on ever more sophisticated applications in new-media technologies. Digital TV technology, for instance, is now almost indistinguishable from computer-networked internet forms. In both cases, advances in user interface technologies have provided greater scope for interactivity, with 'press the red button on your remote control' becoming a part of digital-TV parlance.

Technological convergence has occurred in media production, distribution and consumption. At the production level, text, music, audio and video content are all able to be generated using a standard networked computer. And yet before the digital age of convergence (the wheels were set in motion no more than 20 years ago), these media forms had physically distinct properties and so had to be produced on separate recording formats. As far as distribution goes, traditional forms (import and export, satellite and cable transmission, etc) still operate, but increasingly the global reach of the internet is becoming the focus for multimedia distributors – as well as advertisers. And, of course, digital convergence plays an increasingly important role in consumer experiences. Rapid advancements in digital-TV technology are a clear response to internet usage threatening the domestic dominance of TV (digital and analogue) in recent years.

REMEDIATION

According to American media theorists Jay David Bolter and Richard Grusin in *Remediation* (2000), new media 'remediate' old media. That is to say, new media appropriate 'the techniques, forms and social significance of other media and attempt to rival or refashion them in the name of the real'.[24] So media only become *new* when they can provide something genuinely different from what already exists. New media must be for real! One well-known example of remediation lies in the practice of music-industry back-cataloguing. When the CD became the dominant format for recorded music in the early 1990s, the major record companies promptly remediated their back catalogues of vinyl and cassette recordings onto CD in the expectation that consumers would buy these 'new', 'digitally remastered' versions of what they already owned. And countless consumers did just that! The CD provided better, more authentic, more 'real' sound quality than ever before. While not so widespread, the development of online technologies over the last decade (discussed later) has led to similar processes of musical remediation.

What does remediation tell us about new media? To answer this question, we need to consider two other processes discussed by Bolter and Grusin: immediacy and hypermediacy. Immediacy is the mediated process which seeks to provide 'a window on the world'. The aim is absolute transparency and the disappearance of the artificial processes that make up the media in technological terms. Throughout history, new-media technologies have often pitched their qualities in line with immediacy. The moving images of cinema, for instance, were more immediate than photographic media. But other forms of new media play up their capacity for hypermediacy, mediating overtly constructed and staged representations like rock music productions. Although immediacy and hypermediacy have these different effects, Bolter and Grusin argue that both processes seek to remediate an authentic experience (whether this be the authentic realism of immediacy or the authentic spectacle of hypermediacy). So the remediating promise kept by all new media is to give a bona fide impression or expression of actual people and events.

In *The Language of New Media* (2001), Russian media theorist Lev Manovich adopts a similar view on the 'newness' of new media, though reversing the remediation approach. He is interested not in how new has changed old, but in how old has shaped new – and more specifically, how cinematic heritage has shaped digital film and media. Manovich compares the history and theory of cinema with recent technical and aesthetic developments in new media. And he concludes that there is nothing intrinsically new about digital technologies. Indeed, he draws parallels between new-media post-production techniques like composite imaging and the age-old cinematic technique of montage. Likewise, computer-generated filmic imagery may look more visually stunning than ever before, but it is actually quite a tiny advance on established traditions of animation and cinematography. Manovich's main point is that digital cinema is a continuation of the history of moving-image media rather than a revolutionary innovation. So new media offer a new language, not a new experience altogether, even though digital, computerised forms do make for exciting steps in the evolution of film language.

WEB 2.0

At some point in the early years of the twenty-first century, the web changed direction. Much like Manovich's view of cinema, the language of the web altered for good. For argument's sake, let's say the year was 2004. The period from 1993 – when the web first wove its way into people's lives – to 2003 is known as 'web 1.0'. This was the pioneering age of web design, HTML encoding, unwieldy browsers like Netscape Navigator (superseded by Microsoft's Internet Explorer) and increasingly sophisticated search-engine tools (pre-Google). However, web 1.0 was mostly a space for reading and browsing – due to limited bandwidth, even audio and video content was impractical at first. And producing web content demanded skills in computer programming before the availability of user-friendly software like Dreamweaver. So web 1.0 was an exciting development – but it became a somewhat exclusive haven for technological geeks and millionaire hobbyists. The bursting of the dot-com bubble in 2000 signalled the end of many e-commerce start-ups and revealed the problems of a web offering no major departure from existing commercial or leisure provision.

But by 2004 or thereabouts, the web 2.0 revolution had kicked into gear. Thanks to new applications like wikis, web-logs (blogs), folksonomies and social-networking sites, web 2.0 enabled ordinary users to write, post and publish content without the need for special software. The most popular websites today are all products of web 2.0. YouTube and Flickr are good examples of folksonomies – social-tagging sites allowing users to upload, index, search out and view their own content collaboratively. Facebook, Bebo and MySpace are hugely popular social-networking sites, allowing users to personalise their own profiles, generate audio-visual content, play games, join various groups and networks, and make connections with other users, whether they be strangers or 'old flames' from the distant past. Blog sites are much more scattered and disparate – according to estimates, there are at least 8.5 million floating around cyberspace. Wikis, on the other hand, are the stuff of Wikipedia most notably. Wikis are open web pages that allow users to edit (as well as track the editing of other users) and amend their content. All these applications make web 2.0 a more dynamic and democratic beast than its predecessor.

The endless choice served up by web 2.0, internet economist Chris Anderson claims, is creating unlimited demand for almost anything and everything. In *The Long Tail* (2006), Anderson identifies 'a market of multitudes' in the near-infinite range of products supplied by Amazon, eBay and the like. In web 2.0-speak, more is definitely not less. Rather than traditional mass media and blockbuster films, today's networked media provide a mass of niche products sourced from all kinds of producers and distributors – big and small. What this means for economics is nothing less than breathtaking. If the sum total of all those millions and millions of niche products can out-sell a select few 'hits' that receive all the marketing expenditure, then web 2.0 effectively flings the door wide open to a new, 'flexi-choice', consumer-led sales model for twenty-first-century media and entertainment industries. Instead of the Information Age, enter the Age of Recommendation.

But not everyone is a web 2.0 fan. Critics argue that user-generated new media allow misinformation and the cult of amateurism to flourish. In *The Cult of the Amateur* (2007), American internet critic Andrew Keen argues that 'today's media is shattering the world into a billion personalised truths, each seemingly equally valid and worthwhile'.[25] Keen claims that blogs often amount to veiled corporate propaganda peddled by bogus individuals; that YouTube is a site of anarchy wherein anyone can broadcast their camcorder footage with scant regard for professional ethics or media regulations; that Wikipedia reflects the wisdom of the mob (in contrast to the specialist knowledge gathered into the *Encyclopaedia Britannica*); and that Google's algorithmic logic has become the answer to everything. Part of the problem for Keen is the anonymity of web 2.0. Another nameless amateur video becomes a YouTube hit; nondescript authors find banal readers in the blogosphere; and sexual predators masquerade as friends on social-networking sites. Second Life is perhaps the ultimate expression of Keen's cult of amateurish anonymity and childish escapism. To be anonymous is to be unaccountable for one's content – a worrying diversion from long-standing principles of personal responsibility and identification.

So web 2.0 may not be as desirable as first appearances suggest. It is also debatable whether web 2.0 is really more democratic and user-driven than web 1.0. Interestingly, the internet entrepreneurs of the 1990s had web 2.0 ideals close to their hearts from the outset. The man who invented the World Wide Web, British computer scientist Tim Berners-Lee, conceived it to be a pool of human knowledge that would enable remote individuals to embark on common projects. The web, in theory at least, was designed to provide boundless information that could be universally recognised and retrieved. It was on this basis that various web communities came together on message boards and other forums to share ideas, advice and sometimes even ownership of their particular corner of cyberspace.

For example, eBay in its former guise, AuctionWeb (1995–7), depended heavily on community ideals of sharing and exchanging knowledge. AuctionWeb was a genuine user-to-user site wherein buyers and sellers could assist each other by answering technical queries, providing instructions on how to use certain goods, revising each other's listings for improved accuracy and so on. AuctionWeb's success was also down to the democratic principle that items always sold at prices truly reflecting the point where supply met demand (i.e. at the final-bid figure). Customer service was self-fulfilling. So the collaborative moment claimed by the user-generated web 2.0 has, in fact, a longer and perhaps more convincing history.

CITIZEN JOURNALISM

Citizen journalism is another outcome of new-media convergence and web 2.0. A citizen journalist does not work for a news organisation or have any recognised training in media production, but they are on hand at the scene to report and record a dramatic or notable event. In this sense, the citizen journalist figure is congratulated by some commentators for their independence and the fact they have no axe to grind. The 'gatekeeper' role of traditional news editors is circumvented by the citizen journalist who freely broadcasts news via blogs, YouTube or other unregulated means. Other terms used to describe citizen journalism are backpack journalism, participatory journalism and the blogging reporter. There is even a Mobile Journalist Workstation (MJW), complete with laptop, digital camcorder, headset and satellite phone – unsurprisingly, undercover investigative journalism is not yet possible for the MJW-equipped backpacker! But lest we poke too much fun at citizen journalists who look like freaks of nature, the fact is that Joe Blogger and his roaming camcorder have supplied remarkable news footage to broadcasters that is then instantaneously beamed across global media systems.

Recent examples of spectacular citizen journalism helped to shed light on the horrors of the 2004 Asian tsunami and the 7/7 London terrorist attacks. Mobile-phone cameras, for instance, captured many of the images used by news organisations in their reports on the London bombings. Within six hours of the attacks, the BBC had received over 1,000 photos, 4,000 text messages and 20,000 emails from concerned citizens, perhaps unaware of their key roles in recording historical (and legal) evidence of the events they had witnessed. When a major broadcaster resorts to citizen journalism as a means of reporting a breaking news event, there is the need for a whole new definition of journalism in theory and practice. For every exponent of citizen journalism, however, there's a staunch opponent – not least the professionally trained journalist unable to find a steady job. Critics fear that the painstaking reputations for factual reporting built up by international news agencies like Reuters over hundreds of years may go to waste if broadcasters and citizens form an unhealthy, unprofessional alliance.

PIRACY, P2P, IPOD CULTURE

With the corporate expansion of online music distribution since the turn of the millennium, the internet is now the most important medium for the future of the music industry. In its early years, though, downloading of MP3 (compressed digital music) files via the internet was considered to be a subversive practice, not least by the major record companies who soon filed law suits against heavy uploaders. Peer-to-peer (P2P) file-sharing software enabled users to search out unprecedented libraries of music on sites like Napster – now operating legally and owned by Fortune 100 US electronics retailer Best Buy – and download tracks free of charge and without restriction (given that copyright laws had been flouted). Internet music piracy via new-media technology soon grew to become a major concern for record companies and artists alike. Unlike previous music-piracy activities that had begun operating on the black market in developing economies, internet piracy spread firstly in North America and Europe, therefore hitting the major record companies in their core markets.

So the new-media-enabled P2P technologies behind MP3 file-sharing effectively weakened the traditional divide between producers (industry) and consumers (audience), and forced a transformation in the circulation of media products – not just music, but films, computer games, TV and a whole range of other content threatened by internet piracy. Today, the use of P2P software, although still far from lawful, has become normalised and is perceived, on the whole, to be less of an industry concern – though more advanced applications are developing rapidly to effectively replenish user desire for free goods and services. Nonetheless, the complementary Apple iTunes, iPod and iPhone applications prove the capacity of corporate interests to buy into new-media use and maximise profits from early and late adopters of MP3 technology. Despite Apple's success, however, P2P pirates can take comfort from the thought that it was their innovative and resistant (and criminal) ways that have brought greater flexibility and choice to music-media use, production and distribution.

REFERENCE MATERIALS

Here are several lists of media studies books and websites. The first section comprises references to a selection of seminal studies discussed in this book. Most of these studies have been subsequently republished in more recent editions (dates refer to English-language first editions, unless stated otherwise). Alongside the reference materials detailed here, you should aim to keep in touch with a wide range of local, national and international media output on TV, radio, the internet, and in newspapers and magazines, as well as following developments in the film, music, gaming, advertising, public relations and telecommunications industries. Try not to overuse or underuse any single medium; try to maintain a cross-industry working knowledge of the media – and try to find time for study too (if you can).

SELECTIVE BIBLIOGRAPHY

Anderson, Chris, *The Long Tail: How Endless Choice is Creating Unlimited Demand*, London: Random House, 2006

Ang, Ien, *Watching Dallas: Soap Opera and the Melodramatic Imagination*, London: Methuen, 1985

Baudrillard, Jean, *Simulacra and Simulation*, Michigan: University of Michigan Press, 1994

Bell, Daniel, *The Coming of Post-industrial Society: A Venture in Social Forecasting*, New York: Basic Books, 1973

Bolter, Jay David and Grusin, Richard, *Remediation: Understanding New Media*, Massachusetts: The MIT Press, 2000

Boorstin, Daniel, *The Image: A Guide to Pseudo-events in America*, New York: Atheneum, 1961

Castells, Manuel, *The Rise of the Network Society*, Oxford: Blackwell, 1996

Cohen, Stanley, *Folk Devils and Moral Panics: The Creation of the Mods and Rockers*, London: MacGibbon and Kee, 1972

Davies, Nick, *Flat Earth News*, London: Chatto and Windus, 2008

Dyer, Richard, *Stars*, London: BFI, 1979

Fiske, John, *Understanding Popular Culture*, Boston: Unwin Hyman, 1989

Hall, Stuart et al (eds), *Culture, Media, Language: Working Papers in Cultural Studies 1972–79*, London: Hutchinson, 1980

Hebdige, Dick, *Subculture: The Meaning of Style*, London: Methuen, 1979

Herman, Edward, and Chomsky, Noam, *Manufacturing Consent: The Political Economy of the Mass Media*, New York: Pantheon Books, 1988

Jenkins, Henry, *Textual Poachers: Television Fans and Participatory Culture*, New York: Routledge, 1992

Johnson, Steven, *Everything Bad is Good for You: How Popular Culture is Making Us Smarter*, London: Allen Lane, 2005

Keen, Andrew, *The Cult of the Amateur: How Today's Internet is Killing Our Culture and Assaulting Our Economy*, London: Nicholas Brealey, 2007

Klapper, Joseph, *The Effects of Mass Communication*, New York: The Free Press, 1960

McLuhan, Marshall, *Understanding Media: The Extensions of Man*, New York: McGraw-Hill, 1964

Manovich, Lev, *The Language of New Media*, Massachusetts: The

MIT Press, 2001

Meyrowitz, Joshua, *No Sense of Place: The Impact of Electronic Media on Social Behaviour*, New York: Oxford University Press, 1985

Neale, Stephen, *Genre*, London: BFI, 1980

Postman, Neil, *Amusing Ourselves to Death: Public Discourse in the Age of Show Business*, New York: Penguin, 1985

Rojek, Chris, *Celebrity*, London: Reaktion Books, 2001

Schiller, Herbert, *Mass Communications and American Empire*, New York: AM Kelley, 1969

Tapscott, Don and Williams, Anthony D, *Wikinomics: How Mass Collaboration Changes Everything*, New York: Portfolio, 2006

Thompson, John, *The Media and Modernity: A Social Theory of the Media*, Cambridge: Polity, 1995

Williams, Raymond, *Television: Technology and Cultural Form*, London: Fontana, 1974

Williamson, Judith, *Decoding Advertisements: Ideology and Meaning in Advertising*, London: Marion Boyars, 1978

INTRODUCTORY BOOKS

Abercrombie, Nicholas and Longhurst, Brian, *The Penguin Dictionary of Media Studies*, London: Penguin, 2007

Balnaves, Mark et al, *Media Theories and Approaches: A Global Perspective*, Basingstoke: Palgrave Macmillan, 2008

Bignell, Jonathan, *Media Semiotics: An Introduction*, Manchester: Manchester University Press, 2002 (Second edition)

Branston, Gill and Stafford, Roy, *The Media Student's Book*, Abingdon: Routledge, 2006 (Fourth edition)

Briggs, Asa and Burke, Peter, *A Social History of the Media: From Gutenberg to the Internet*, Cambridge: Polity, 2005 (Second edition)

Bryant, Jennings and Thompson, Susan, *Fundamentals of Media*

Effects, New York: McGraw-Hill, 2002

Buckingham, David, *Media Education: Literacy, Learning and Contemporary Culture*, Cambridge: Polity, 2003

Connell, Barbara (ed), *Exploring the Media: Text, Industry, Audience*, Leighton Buzzard: Auteur, 2008

Couldry, Nick, *Inside Culture: Reimagining the Method of Cultural Studies*, London: Sage, 2000

Curran, James and Seaton, Jean, *Power without Responsibility: The Press and Broadcasting in Britain*, Abingdon: Routledge, 2003 (Sixth edition)

Devereux, Eoin, *Understanding the Media*, London: Sage, 2007 (Second edition)

Gane, Nicholas and Beer, David, *New Media: The Key Concepts*, Oxford: Berg, 2008

Gauntlett, David, *Media, Gender and Identity: An Introduction*, Abingdon: Routledge, 2008 (Second edition)

Gibson, Janine, *Media 08: The Essential Guide to the Changing Media Landscape*, London: Guardian Newspapers, 2008

Hall, Stuart (ed), *Representation: Cultural Representations and Signifying Practices*, London: Sage, 1997

Hesmondhalgh, David, *The Cultural Industries*, London: Sage, 2007 (Second edition)

Laughey, Dan, *Key Themes in Media Theory*, New York: Open University Press/McGraw-Hill, 2007

McQuail, Denis, *McQuail's Mass Communication Theory*, London: Sage, 2005 (Fifth edition)

Moores, Shaun, *Media/Theory: Thinking about Media and Communications*, Abingdon: Routledge, 2005

Storey, John, *Cultural Theory and Popular Culture: An Introduction*, Harlow: Pearson Education, 2006 (Fourth edition)

Webster, Frank, *Theories of the Information Society*, Abingdon: Routledge, 2006 (Third edition)

WEBSITES

Advertising Standards Authority – www.asa.org.uk (Independent body that oversees advertising codes of practice and research on media trends)

British Broadcasting Corporation – www.bbc.co.uk

British Film Institute – www.bfi.org.uk

Channel 4 Media News – www.channel4.com/news/arts_entertainment/media

Chartered Institute of Public Relations – www.cipr.co.uk (Professional body that oversees public relations codes of practice as well as training, research and publications)

English and Media Centre – www.englishandmedia.co.uk (Resources and publications intended for school teachers and students)

Guardian Media News – www.guardian.co.uk/media

Higher Education Academy: Art Design Media Subject Centre – www.adm.heacademy.ac.uk (Resources, live issues and publications for media education, learning and teaching)

Index on Censorship – www.indexoncensorship.org (Independent organisation that promotes freedom of expression in the media and other sectors)

Indymedia – www.indymedia.org.uk (Alternative media site offering non-commercial, grassroots coverage of social and political news)

International Association for Media and Communication Research – www.iamcr.org

Internet Movie Database – www.imdb.com (Comprehensive information on films and TV shows)

Media and Communications Studies – www.aber.ac.uk/media

Media and Social Theory Site – www.theory.org.uk

Media, Communication and Cultural Studies Association – www.meccsa.org.uk

Media Ed – www.mediaed.org.uk (Media teaching resources and ideas)

Media Education Association – www.mediaedassociation.org.uk

Media Literacy and Technology in Education – www.understandmedia.com

Media Studies Coursework and Exam Revision Resources – www.mediaedu.co.uk

Media UK – www.mediauk.com (Directory for the media industries)

Media Week – www.mediaweek.co.uk (Business magazine for the commercial media sector)

National Media Museum – www.nationalmediamuseum.org.uk

Office of Communications – www.ofcom.org.uk (Independent regulator and competition authority for the media and communications industries)

Press Complaints Commission – www.pcc.org.uk (Independent body that oversees journalism codes of practice and investigates complaints about the editorial content of newspapers and magazines)

Society for Cinema and Media Studies – www.cmstudies.org

UCAS – www.ucas.com (Directory listing all UK Higher Education courses in media studies and related subjects)

Undercurrents – www.undercurrents.org (Alternative media site focusing on non-mainstream issues around social and environmental justice)

NOTES

1   McLuhan, Marshall, *Understanding Media: The Extensions of Man*, New York: McGraw-Hill (1964), p.8

2   Postman, Neil, *Amusing Ourselves to Death: Public Discourse in the Age of Show Business*, New York: Penguin (1985), p.76

3   Meyrowitz, Joshua, *No Sense of Place: The Impact of Electronic Media on Social Behaviour*, New York: Oxford University Press (1985), p.67

4   McLuhan, Marshall, *Understanding Media: The Extensions of Man*, New York: McGraw-Hill (1964), p.8

5   Buckingham, David, *Children Talking Television: The Making of Television Literacy*, London: Falmer Press (1993), p.269

6   Adorno, Theodor and Horkheimer, Max, *Dialectic of Enlightenment*, London: Allen Lane (1972), p.137

7   Schiller, Herbert, *Mass Communications and American Empire*, New York: AM Kelley (1969), p.124

8   Liebes, Tamar and Katz, Elihu, *The Export of Meaning: Cross-cultural Readings of Dallas*, New York: Oxford University Press (1990), p.75

9   Barthes, Roland, *Mythologies*, London: Vintage Books (1957), p.116

10 Boorstin, Daniel, *The Image: A Guide to Pseudo-events in America*, New York: Atheneum (1961), p.11

11   Jameson, Fredric, *Postmodernism or, The Cultural Logic of Late Capitalism*, London: Verso (1991), p.10

12   Baudrillard, Jean, *Simulations*, New York: Semiotext(e) (1983), p.25

13   Baudrillard, Jean, *The Spirit of Terrorism, and Requiem for the Twin Towers*, London: Verso (2002), pp.27, 29

14   Toffler, Alvin, *The Third Wave*, London: Pan (1980), p.170

15   Ibid, p.176

16   Bell, Daniel, *The Coming of Post-industrial Society: A Venture in Social Forecasting*, New York: Basic Books (1973), p.188

17   Ibid, p.119

18   Cohen, Stanley, *Folk Devils and Moral Panics: The Creation of the Mods and Rockers*, London: MacGibbon and Kee (1972), p.1

19   Ibid, p.2

20   Dyer, Richard, *Stars*, London: BFI (1979), p.38

21   Fiske, John, *Understanding Popular Culture*, Boston: Unwin Hyman (1989), p.172

22   Jenkins, Henry, *Textual Poachers: Television Fans and Participatory Culture*, New York: Routledge (1992), pp.23–24

23   Neale, Stephen, *Genre*, London: BFI (1980), p.19

24   Bolter, Jay David and Grusin, Richard, *Remediation: Understanding New Media*, Massachusetts: The MIT Press (2000), p.65

25   Keen, Andrew, *The Cult of the Amateur: How Today's Internet is Killing Our Culture and Assaulting Our Economy*, London: Nicholas Brealey (2007), p.17

INDEX

SHORT FILMS
...how to make and distribute them

NATHAN PARKER

Nathan Parker looks at: development of initial idea – screenwriting processes – location scouting – budgets – casting – shooting formats – directing – post-production – editing – computer effects – soundtracks – how to get your short film distributed – international film festivals.

With additional interviews with experienced professionals on all aspects of short film making and production, and a bonus DVD featuring five award-winning short films discussed as case studies in the book, layouts for budget spreadsheets, release forms, contracts and more...

Nathan Parker is a filmmaker and teaches courses in short filmmaking and cinematography at Central Saint Martins in London.

ARTS REVIEWS
...and how to write them

CELIA BRAYFIELD

The most wanted, the most feared, the most hated, the most powerful job in journalism: being a reviewer means writing about something you love and getting paid for it. So for a lot of people it's the No 1 dream job in the media. Whether your passion is film, music, books, visual arts or the stage, you can get closer to it as a reviewer and establish a career in one of the most influential roles open to a writer. Get the edge on the competition with a book that's a treasure trove of wisdom, experience and downright cunning, passed on by the best critics writing today.

This book explains how to seize your readers' attention and how to be witty always, fascinating most of the time and bitchy when you need to be. We look back at the history of the critic and some of the groundbreaking groups who have shaped our culture, including Dorothy Parker and the Algonquin Round Table, the French New Wave directors who founded *Les Cahiers du Cinema* and London's celebrated *Modern Review*, founded by Julie Burchill, Toby Young and Cosmo Landesman.

£9.99   978-1-904048-91-6 paperback   B (198 X 129mm)
160pp World Rights

To order your copy

£9.99 including free postage and packing
(UK and Republic of Ireland only)
£10.99 for overseas orders

For credit card orders phone 0207 430 1021 (ref MS)

For orders by post – cheques payable to
Oldcastle Books
21 Great Ormond Street
London WC1N 3JB
www.kamerabooks.co.uk